THE RUNNER'S COACH

Cedarwinds Publishing Company

THE RUNNER'S COACH

A Scientific Approach to Modern Endurance Training

Roy T. Benson

Cedarwinds Publishing Company

This book is dedicated, with love, to Betty

THE RUNNER'S COACH

Published by Cedarwinds Publishing Company
P.O. Box 13618
Tallahassee, Florida 32317
Orders: 800/548-2388
Editorial: 850/224-9261
Fax: 850/561-0747

Library of Congress Cataloging in
Publication Data

Benson, Roy T. 1941-
Runner's Coach, The
796.42—dc20 1. Running. 2. Running —Training. I. title
ISBN 0-915297-12-4

1st printing   June, 1994
2nd printing   October, 1997

V 10 9 8 7 6 5 4 3 2

Contents

Charts, Forms and Illustrations

1. The Concept of Individualization

The Runner's Coach has only one goal: to teach runners and coaches, respectively, how to select for themselves or each of their runners the appropriate workouts for any given day, at any given phase of training.

The Runner's Coach has only one foundation: the science of exercise physiology. I am not writing about the Art of Coaching. That's the poetic way of referring to how I apply the principles of science to each and every one of my different athletes each and every day. I'm a pretty good artist today now that I have had 31 years of experience as a coach. But, back when I was a rookie coach, had I had access to the scientific body of knowledge that is currently available, I could have spent a hell of a lot less time learning the artist's brush strokes. In short, this little manual is simply my explanation of how to become an applied exercise physiologist who works with runners. Combine these lessons with a little experience and you, too, can practice both the art and science of coaching.

To be honest, I must admit that this book would not have been possible just a few years ago. Until, recently it was simply not practical to base training on the science of the cardiac response to exercise. No runner was going to stop in the middle of every workout every few minutes to count his or her pulse. Sure, they were only too eager to stop after each repeat of an interval workout for a pulse check. But that was obviously just to delay the inevitable resumption of the workout, to

1

gain just an extra bit of recovery time. But out on the roads during easy or tempo runs, forget it.

Now, however, heart monitors finally make my approach easy to practice. We're already into the fifth generation of telemetric (wireless) monitors. They're small, comfortable, water-proof and user friendly. Above all, they're now actually cheaper than some running shoes.

WAIT! Don't stop reading! If you think that this is going to be only about training with a heart monitor, you're wrong.

You don't win a race by crossing the finish line with the lowest heart rate. Time still counts. So, pace per mile is the other part of my philosophy of coaching. But this, too, is based on exercise physiology research; thus, I'm relying heavily here on a marriage of the stop watch and the heart monitor. What we then get is a realistic way to measure how hard a runner is working *as well as* a way of knowing if he or she is training intelligently.

As both a runner and coach, I used to find the challenge of selecting workouts overwhelmingly complicated. There is a bewildering variety of choices. Hundreds of books and thousands of articles offer readers as many different workouts. But few answer the ultimate question: what exact workout would be of the absolute most benefit to me right here, right now, on this day?

Consider the possible variables that constitute a single workout:

1. the total distance
2. the pace of each segment
3. the distance of the repeats
4. the length of the recovery interval

5. the general type of workout:
   a. Long Slow Distance
   b. steady state
   c. anaerobic threshold (AT)
   d. fartlek
   e. intervals
   f. speed work
   g. lactate threshold
6. the current "phase" of training
7. the duration of the training cycle (i.e., 7-day, 10-day, 14-day, etc.)

All of the above items are just another way of asking, "How long, how hard, how fast or slow, and how often should I run?"

Complicating things further is the fact that there is no standard training language. It seems that anyone who has ever expressed a written opinion has invented his or her own pet names for certain common workouts, occasionally even giving new names to those few labels that have become more or less universally agreed upon.

Although the *Runner's Coach* can't impose a universal language on the sport, it can teach you how to select the right workout, in a very user-friendly fashion.

So, how do coaches and runners really know if the workouts they pick will accomplish the particular conditioning goal that should be behind the design and execution of every single workout?

It seems to me, since nearly everyone readily acknowledges that each runner is different, we can also agree each runner's workout somehow must be different. Or, better yet, might it simply be that the same workout should be run differently by each runner?

How? My answer is to design a workout according to each runner's level of ability and current level of fitness. In short: *just vary the pace that each runner does the same workout.*

For example, Mary just ran a 5,000 meter race in 18:18 while Bill finished in 21:11. In their next major interval workout, they both could do 12 x 400 meters with a 70% recovery interval, but Mary should be running considerably faster than Bill. Her 400's should be done in 1:25.5 seconds, while Bill should run each 400 in 1:38.2, assuming that they each are hoping to improve a little in their next race.

How did I come up with those times, you ask. Hint: see the Pace and Effort Chart on page 15 (or Appendix B) to locate their current 5k times in the second column from the left. Then note the training paces required in Phase III to bring about the 90-95% level of EFFORT needed to achieve optimal improvement. Mary and Bill's differences accepted, then the only thing that these two runners should have in common is that they are *both working just as hard.*

These percentages of effort should not be confused with percentages of maximum heart rate, although they are related. See page eight (or Appendix A), to note the relationship between percentage of EFFORT and Target Heart Rates.)

Effort Based Training (EBT) is what I call my approach. I've used it to coach middle and long distance runners since the first time that I palpated a runner's carotid artery back during the 70's glory days of the Florida Track Club in Gainesville, Florida. In my curiosity to find out what was really going on inside all those outstanding graduate and undergraduate runners at the University of Florida, I took to counting heart rates. Back then I assumed, and was indeed assured by my physiology professor, Dr. Chris Zauner, that a runner's effort could best be measured by checking the RPM's of his engine, i.e., his heart rate.

Heart rates, I also discovered, were a better way to individualize workouts. So, for the last 23 out of my 31 years as a coach at the military, high school, university, club, and now the private levels, I have been trying to figure out the best way to calculate target heart rates as the basis for preparing and executing EBT workouts.

EBT is a simple system I've empirically and scientifically developed to measure if a runner is working out at the correct pace. But it doesn't use only time per distance as the unit of measurement. It also relates your heart rate to your running effort. And consequently your heart rate becomes the primary gauge by which we plan and measure all workouts.

Effort, in this sense, is a numerical index expressed as a percentage of a fit person's all-out, drop-dead-as-you-cross-the-finish-line capacity for exertion.

One way to explain EBT is to compare it to traditional methods of prescribing workouts. For example: It's Saturday and the traditional coach wants you to do a three mile AT (anaerobic threshold) run at 15 to 20 seconds per mile slower than your current 10km race pace. There are several things that could be wrong with this plan. You may not have an accurate estimate of your current 10km fitness because your latest races have been on really hilly, slow courses. You may be feeling bad (tired and/or hung over) this particular Saturday morning. The IRS may have just announced that your tax return was incorrect and you owe them more money. The weather or terrain may be out of the ordinary. All these factors and many others could affect the level of effort necessary to keep the traditional coach happy with the time you take to do the workout.

On the other hand, a coach who uses EBT would approach this situation differently. She would say that she wants her runner to go out and run for 15 to 20 minutes at 80 to 85% effort. This coach doesn't really care how much distance her runner covers during that time interval. Likewise she is not all that concerned about the elapsed time it takes to travel a given distance. She saves that kind of concern for races and time trials. This is training. The coach is merely concerned with the level of effort and keeping it constant during the time of the run.

Think about it for a moment. In the traditional way of coaching, the stopwatch becomes the Almighty. It's this tick-tock mechanism that tells us whether or not the workout was done "right," often leading to confusion about a lot of factors, including a runner's mental toughness. This traditional methodology ignores the fact that it is carefully orchestrated "effort" and not time-per-unit of distance that maximizes the body's adaptation process, while at the same time preventing injuries. Thanks to telemetric heart monitors and EBT, all this is changing.

So, let's see how we can now use the heart monitor as a tachometer to observe exactly how our engine is running.

Individualizing Your Target Heart Rates

Monitoring your heart rate is the best way to get precise feedback about what your body thinks about today's workout. To get constant, reliable feedback, I recommend using a Heart Rate Monitor. So far the telemetry technology developed by Polar is unmatched by any other pulse monitors and that's why I include a Polar monitor in each and every package of coaching services that I provide my clients. The key to successful workouts is having a good set of target heart rates.

If your goal for the days's easy run is to recover at a 60% to 65% level of effort, for example, in what range should you keep your heart rate? 125-132 beats per minute? 137-145? For you at your current great level of fitness, the answer might be 122-129 BPM (beats per minute), but for your younger running partner, 132-141 BPM might be appropriate. You have to know several facts before you can tell if you should run together.

First, to use effort-based training effectively, you must know your Maximum Heart Rate (MHR). You can identify this either by actual laboratory testing (the most accurate way) or by using the Predicted Maximum Heart Rate Axis in the accompanying Target Heart Rate Calculator. But using the MHR alone does not account for individual levels of fitness. In fact, it penalizes fitter runners, whose hearts are stronger and work more efficiently, by making them run harder than they should. And beginning runners, just starting to get in shape, may not be working hard enough to get their sought-after training effect.

To help you target your training heart rates more accurately without a lot of math, Ned Frederick, Larry

Simpson and I have designed a Training Heart Rate Calculator (see pages 13 and 14). that takes your fitness level into account. This utilizes the great work on target heart rates done by the Finnish physiologist, M.L. Karvonen.

To use our copyrighted calculator, you just need to know two things: 1) Your resting heart rate, which indicates your basic level of fitness, and 2) your Maximum Heart Rate, actual or predicted. Before learning how to use the calculator, you need to determine these two figures first.

Your resting heart rate gives a good indication of your basic fitness level. The more well-conditioned your body, the stronger your heart muscles and the greater the capacity of your heart's chambers. That means a lower than average resting heart rate. For example, the average resting heart rate for sedentary men is 72 BPM and for women, 84 beats per minute. But an average "chronically fit" male runner might be more likely to have a resting heart rate in the low 40's, and a "chronically fit" woman's rate might be well below 60 beats per minute. So, fit people need credit for their condition. It's one of the major payoffs for all that hard work and remember: lower heart rates make your hair last longer!

Determining your resting heart rate is easy: put on your heart monitor as soon as you wake up in the morning for several days in a row. Lie back down for a few minutes to see how low you can get your reading. Average the readings you get and that's your Resting Heart Rate (RHR).

But how about your Maximum Heart Rate (MHR)? What is your "drop-dead-from-exhaustion-at-the-finish-line" rate? There are two ways to determine it: 1) have it tested by a cardiologist or trained exercise technician, or 2) use your predicted maximum from a formula.

Although it can be expensive, the most accurate way to determine your individual MHR is to have it clinically tested by a specialist who knows how to administer a true *maximal* stress test on a treadmill. (Don't take the test on a bicycle ergometer.) This means that the specialist lets you (or rather *makes* you) stay on the treadmill until you absolutely can not keep up your pace anymore and are in danger of falling off the back of the treadmill. By this time, your heart rate should have leveled off and refused to go any higher despite your urgently increasing state of exhaustion. Another informal way of "maxing out" is in an actual running "time trial" supervised by a trained coach or exercise physiologist. Knowing your actual maximum rate will enable you to tailor your workouts to your physical condition as closely as possible.

For some people, including the five to 10% of the population whose MHR's are above or below average predictions by as much as 12 to 24 BPM, testing may be worth the money it costs. If you choose to be tested, be sure to have the tests done by trained professionals. Don't try any do-it-yourself time trials; the emergency room is not a desirable finish line.

For most people who don't have the money or time to get tested, using the Predicted Maximum Heart Rate approach will be more popular. Since much recent research has shown that the old formula of 220 minus your age isn't that accurate for younger, older and chronically fit people, our Training Heart Rate Calculator has been designed to take the research findings of Hakki, Luger, Pollack, Blair and the new Ball State University study of over 2,010 subjects by Kaminsky et al into account.

Using the Training Heart Rate Calculators on pages 13 and 14 is easy. First forget every formula you've ever seen or tried to memorize! They are all incorporated into the right hand axis of the calculator. *Just find your current age on the outside of the right hand axis. Directly opposite of your age on the inside of the right hand axis is your predicted max heart rate.* Just remember that you may prove to be as much as plus or minus 24 beats per minute above or below average. If so, it won't take you long to realize it when you start training in your THR zones. If common sense tells you that you shouldn't have to run so damn slow at your different zones, or so incredibly fast, then do a correlation test with the pace chart. Get your HR up to 60-65% and time yourself for a mile jog while carefully staying within your THR zone. Then find that time in the 4th column from the left (under the label 60-65%) on the Pace & Effort Chart. Look across to the time listed in next column to the left under the 10K heading. Also, while you're at it, check the next column to the left for your 5K time. You should be able to race 10K & 5K in those two "Y" times, if at 60-65% effort, your pace for a mile was "X." If not, your MHR prediction probably needs adjusting.

If so, use the following suggestions:

1) If you reached your 60-65% THR zone at frustratingly slower paces than your common sense and the pace chart recommend, you need to raise tour PMHR by 12-24 BPM.

2) If you had to run hard as hell to elevate your HR to the target numbers, you probably have a much lower than predicted MHR. Go ahead and lower the age-predicted numbers by 12 to 24 BPM.

Following chapters will give you some precise THR's that will show you how hard, in slightly imprecise THR zones, your body ought to be working. This admission about imprecision is necessary because honesty becomes your coach. Especially one who is also an exercise physiologist and knows that, quite frankly, it is impossible to run a whole workout at exactly one single THR. Furthermore, all good scientists know that each runner's exact capacity for oxygen usage varies with levels of fitness and percent body fat and this the exact percentage of usage varies from person to person. So, to cover the range of possible variations, we simply assign each runner a THR zone because of frequent exceptions we have to make about Predicted Maximum Heart Rates. You will soon see in the following discussion why we waffle worse than a politician about MHR's.

The Training Heart Rate Calculator makes the math part of determining your Target Heart Rates (THR) very simple. It is a state-of-the-art work-of-art that leaves no room for doubt or argument. Just follow the instructions and you're in business.

Now you're ready to put our invention to use developing your very own THR zones. Take a look at the sample chart reproduced above. On the far left is an axis labeled "MRP" for Morning Resting Pulse. On the far right is the axis labeled "MHR" for either Predicted or Actual Max Heart Rate. The percentages shown on the vertical axes in the middle of the chart refer to Karvonen Intensity Levels and represent the amount of effort corresponding to the universal recommendations of coaches about how hard one should work to get in shape.

To find your individual THR zones for various levels, draw a line between your MRP on the left axis and your MHR (whether it's predicted or actual) on the right. Where the line crosses the appropriate intensity lines is the target heart rate you should shoot for during your different workouts from day to day.

For example, let's say that you have a MPR of 51 BPM and a MHR of 195. You want to work out at 60-65% on a real easy, rest & recovery day. Draw your line from 51 on the left to 195 on the right. It crosses the 60% and 65% intensity lines at 138 to 145 BPM. To train at 60-65% requires a pace fast enough to elevate your HR to at least 138, but slow enough so that you don't go over 145 BPM. Although you won't feel that it's easy to run that slow, now at least it's easy to know your target heart rates.

Some caveats: an important conclusion that came out of the recent Ball State study was that females' MHR's are not as high as previously expected. In fact, they are several BPM's lower than the figures for men. In recognition of the this important finding, we have designed a separate Training Heart Rate Calculator for women and publish it here for the first time on page 14.

I have also found quite a few young runners (ages 10-15) that are way off the charts—sometimes as high as 250 BPM at maximum effort! Without knowing your real MHR from treadmill stress testing, you will have to work for a while at correlating your training paces and training heart rates.

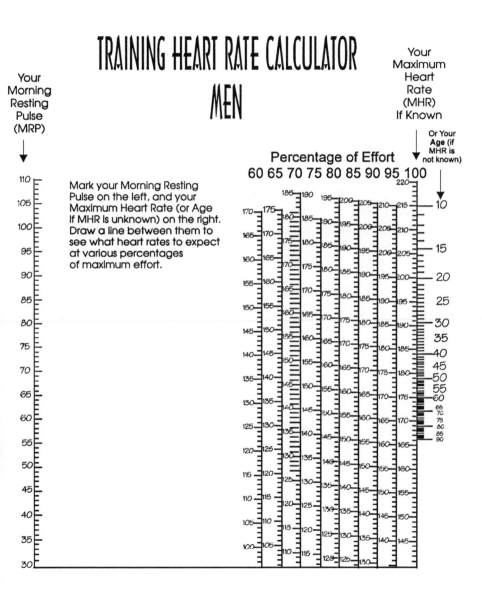

TRAINING HEART RATE CALCULATOR
MEN

Your Morning Resting Pulse (MRP)

Your Maximum Heart Rate (MHR) If Known

Or Your Age (if MHR is not known)

Percentage of Effort

Mark your Morning Resting Pulse on the left, and your Maximum Heart Rate (or Age if MHR is unknown) on the right. Draw a line between them to see what heart rates to expect at various percentages of maximum effort.

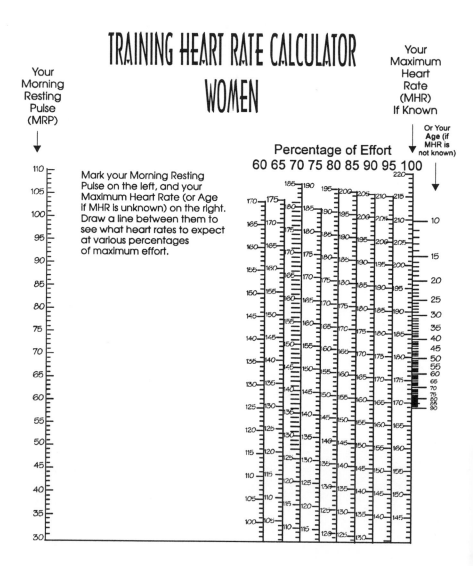

TRAINING HEART RATE CALCULATOR
WOMEN

Your Morning Resting Pulse (MRP)

Your Maximum Heart Rate (MHR) If Known

Or Your **Age** (if MHR is not known)

Percentage of Effort
60 65 70 75 80 85 90 95 100

Mark your Morning Resting Pulse on the left, and your Maximum Heart Rate (or Age if MHR is unknown) on the right. Draw a line between them to see what heart rates to expect at various percentages of maximum effort.

Pace & Effort Chart
For Four Phases of Training

Percentages of Maximum Heart Rate -->			60 to 65%	70 to 75%	80 to 85%	90 to 95%	95 to 100%
If your current mile time is:	Or your current 5K time is:	Or if current 10K time is:	Your Recovery Pace will be: (mile)	Your Phase I Pace will be: (mile)	Your Ph. II Pace will be: (mile)	Your Ph. III Pace will be: (440M)	Your Phase IV Pace will be: (100M)
03:45	13:00 (04:11/mi)	27:00 (04:21/mi)	05:51	05:30	04:42	01:01.9	00:13.0
03:54	13:29 (04:21/mi)	28:00 (04:30/mi)	06:03	05:42	04:52	01:04.1	00:13.4
04:02	13:58 (04:30/mi)	29:00 (04:41/mi)	06:15	05:53	05:02	01:06.2	00:13.8
04:11	14:27 (04:39/mi)	30:00 (04:50/mi)	06:27	06:05	05:11	01:08.3	00:14.2
04:20	14:56 (04:49/mi)	31:00 (05:00/mi)	06:40	06:16	05:21	01:10.5	00:14.6
04:28	15:25 (04:58/mi)	32:00 (05:10/mi)	06:52	06:28	05:31	01:12.6	00:15.1
04:37	15:54 (05:07/mi)	33:00 (05:19/mi)	07:04	06:39	05:41	01:14.8	00:15.6
04:46	16:23 (05:18/mi)	34:00 (05:29/mi)	07:16	06:51	05:51	01:16.9	00:16.0
04:54	16:52 (05:26/mi)	35:00 (05:39/mi)	07:28	07:02	06:00	01:19.1	00:16.5
05:03	17:21 (05:35/mi)	36:00 (05:49/mi)	07:40	07:14	06:10	01:21.2	00:16.9
05:12	17:49 (05:45/mi)	37:00 (05:58/mi)	07:52	07:25	06:20	01:23.3	00:17.4
05:21	18:18 (05:54/mi)	38:00 (06:08/mi)	08:04	07:36	06:30	01:25.5	00:17.8
05:29	18:47 (06:03/mi)	39:00 (06:17/mi)	08:16	07:48	06:39	01:27.6	00:18.3
05:38	19:16 (06:13/mi)	40:00 (06:27/mi)	08:28	07:59	06:49	01:29.7	00:18.7
05:47	19:45 (06:22/mi)	41:00 (06:37/mi)	08:40	08:10	06:59	01:31.8	00:19.1
05:56	20:14 (06:31/mi)	42:00 (06:46/mi)	08:52	08:21	07:09	01:33.9	00:19.6
06:04	20:43 (06:41/mi)	43:00 (06:56/mi)	09:03	08:32	07:18	01:36.1	00:20.0
06:13	21:11 (06:50/mi)	44:00 (07:06/mi)	09:15	08:43	07:28	01:38.2	00:20.5
06:22	21:41 (06:59/mi)	45:00 (07:16/mi)	09:27	08:54	07:37	01:40.3	00:20.9
06:31	22:10 (07:09/mi)	46:00 (07:25/mi)	09:38	09:05	07:47	01:42.5	00:21.4
06:39	22:38 (07:18/mi)	47:00 (07:35/mi)	09:50	09:16	07:56	01:44.6	00:21.8
06:48	23:07 (07:27/mi)	48:00 (07:44/mi)	10:01	09:27	08:06	01:46.7	00:22.2
06:57	23:36 (07:37/mi)	49:00 (07:54/mi)	10:13	09:38	08:15	01:48.8	00:22.6
07:06	24:05 (07:46/mi)	50:00 (08:04/mi)	10:24	09:49	08:25	01:50.9	00:23.1
07:15	24:34 (07:55/mi)	51:00 (08:14/mi)	10:35	10:00	08:34	01:52.9	00:23.5
07:23	25:03 (08:05/mi)	52:00 (08:23/mi)	10:46	10:10	08:44	01:55.0	00:24.0
07:32	25:32 (08:14/mi)	53:00 (08:33/mi)	10:58	10:21	08:53	01:57.1	00:24.4
07:41	26:01 (08:24/mi)	54:00 (08:43/mi)	11:09	10:32	09:02	01:59.1	00:24.8
07:50	26:30 (08:33/mi)	55:00 (08:52/mi)	11:20	10:42	09:12	02:02.4	00:25.5
07:59	26:59 (08:42/mi)	56:00 (09:02/mi)	11:31	10:53	09:21	02:03.3	00:25.7
08:07	27:28 (08:51/mi)	57:00 (09:11/mi)	11:42	11:03	09:30	02:05.3	00:26.1
08:16	27:56 (09:01/mi)	58:00 (09:21/mi)	11:52	11:13	09:39	02:07.4	00:26.5
08:25	28:25 (09:10/mi)	59:00 (09:31/mi)	12:03	11:24	09:48	02:09.4	00:27.0
08:34	28:54 (09:19/mi)	60:00 (09:41/mi)	12:14	11:34	09:57	02:11.4	00:27.4

Compiled by: Larry Simpson
References: Separately published research of J. Daniels & M. J. Karvonen; also Amby Burfoot, ``The Perfect Pace," *Runner's World*

Combining Pace and Effort with Heart Rates

Now I want to explain how the Pace and Effort Chart translates Training Heart Rates into real world workouts and races.

For example, if you are a 34:00 10km runner, or a 16:23 5k runner, then the chart will tell you that a 5:51 per mile pace should elicit an 80 to 85% effort. At this pace and effort, your heart rate should match up with your predicted THR shown for 80% to 85% on the nomograph on page eight.

On my Training Pace and Effort Chart (see page 15) you will find, associated with each of the four phases of training, effort ranges that relate your pace to your training heart rates. One of your challenges will be to assess your current fitness level in order to determine your "individualized" workouts. This will then point you to a Training Plan (see an example on page 19) featuring the right Training Phase. Your daily Training Pattern can then be drawn up using your very own fitness and ability related, individualized, workouts (see the sample on pages 22-23, then make some xeroxes of the blank ones in the Appendix).

How to Make Up Your Training Program

A Training Program is made up of several components which in my system all cleverly have the same initials. The first part is an overall view of where you're going: a Training Plan. This is merely a calendar listing when you plan to do things.

The Training Plan is then broken down into four Training Phases. Once that's done, you can write a

Training Pattern for all of the weeks in each Phase. Patterns are your daily workouts planned down to minute details so you'll know how hard and how much to run.

Training Plans

First, make a commitment! Write down your goal in ink.

Write it right at the bottom of the Training Plan and Race Schedule. To start your planning, xerox a blank plan sheet from the appendix and make a calendar out of the work sheet like I did on the sample on page 19 by writing in the dates of each week during your plan. I prefer to start my weeks on Mondays, but use whatever day you want.

Next I blocked out how long my sample runner was going to spend in each phase of training. You will need to read the chapter on each phase, but assume that I'm writing out a Training Plan for an obviously talented, veteran runner whose goal is to break 15:00 for 5,000 meters. He is just starting back into training after a three week period of active rest. The seasons usually don't fall on the dates that I've used, but let's assume that our runner can live an idealistic life, training all fall to get in shape for a winter racing season that culminates with the Indoor National Championships.

Once I had determined the ideal length of each Training Phase, I then filled in the races to be run during Phase III. In our life-is-perfect sample, I made up a season of races that would be good for preparing a runner to race at 5,000 meters. I was careful not to schedule too many races, preferring instead to keep our runner fresh and eager for competition.

Once the schedule was determined, I filled in the appropriate Saturday workouts between competitions. The way to select them will be explained in each of the respective chapters on the Phases of Training.

Next, I assigned the long runs to be done on Sunday of each week. You'll notice that I like to make the long run short on a day after a race.

To decide how many miles per week to run, I next filled out the M/WK column using fairly conservative totals in an effort to aim for consistency of training, rather than risk injury by going for higher miles. My philosophy is that *frequent* but *moderate* workouts on a *consistent* basis are the key to success.

And finally, I made sure that our runner had adequate rest days by filling in the number of days per week that he is to train.

At this point, let me confess something to you: there is no magic way to know if you're filling out a Training Plan correctly. It simply requires using some judgment while keeping an open mind. You may need to come back and revise your plan if you find that it isn't working. This is known in the coaching trade as the Finagle Factor. In short, be ready to be flexible.

Fall & Winter 1992/93
Training Plan And Race Schedule

WK OF DATE	PHASES	M/WK	DAY/WK	SATURDAY	Sun/LR
Sept. 7		12	4	1 mile steady state	3
14	I	16	5	2 mi. S.S.	4
21		20	5	" " " "	4
28		25	5	3 mi . "	5
Oct. 5		30	5	" " " "	5
12		20	4	" " " "	4
19		30	5	4 " " "	5
26		35	6	5 " " "	7
Nov 2		40	6	2 miles A.T.	8
9	II	35	6	" " "	8
16		45	6	3 miles "	10
23		50	6	" " "	12
30		45	6	" " "	10
Dec 7		40	6	5K RACE	6-7
14		45	6	3 mi A.T.	10
21		35	6	10k RACE	6-7
28		45	6	3 mi A.T.	10
Jan 4		40	5	8k RACE	6-7
11	III	40	6	3 mi A.T.	10
18		35	6	2 mile race	6-7
25		30	5	1 mile race	7-8
Feb 1		40	6	3 mile A.T.	10
8		30	5	5K RACE	5-6
15		30	6	2 mile A.T.	8
22		30	6	800 meter Race	8
Mar 1		25	5	2 mile A.T.	6-7
8		25	5	5K RACE	4-5
15	IV	25	5	2 mile A.T.	6
22		20	4	1,500 m time trial	
29		15	4	Nat'l Indoor Champs	
April 5				5,000 meters	
12				14:56	
19				↑	
26					

goal

The Four Phases of Training

Over these past 31 years, I have identified four separate levels of fitness that an athlete must develop in order to reach peak performance. This leads to the obvious separation of training into different phases. Workouts in each phase then concentrate on developing, pyramid fashion, one level of fitness upon another. Using the laboratory language of the physiologist in me, I call these four phases: Endurance, Stamina, Economy and Speed.

Or using the more familiar locker room language of a coach, I also refer to these four phases as: 1. getting into shape; 2. getting ready to race; 3. competing through the season; 4. coming to a peak.

It is important to pay close attention to your heart rate during training to make sure that it matches the level of effort associated with your particular phase of training. That's next. I'll show you exactly how to do that in the following chapters.

Roy Benson's Four Phases of Training

2. Phase I: Endurance Training

Stop! Hold on right here before you lace up your grippies and rush out the door to try the workouts outlined at the end of this chapter. Before moving a single toe towards the door, you must understand WHY it's so important to stay within the percentages of effort assigned to this phase of training.

Your responsibility as an intelligent, responsible athlete is to accomplish the physiological adaptations listed below before moving on to Phase II. To make these things happen, you must follow the program closely.

Your *endurance* will be developed when these bodily changes have taken place:

1. Your maximum oxygen uptake has begun to improve because your heart, lungs, and muscles have gotten better at absorbing, delivering, and burning lots of molecules of O_2.

2. Your muscles have learned to take the path of least resistance, thereby improving your efficiency. This means that you move your body in a fairly straight line using the least amount of energy possible.

3. Your muscles have learned how to metabolize fat more efficiently and have become, in the immortal words of *Fit or Fat* author Covert Bailey, "better butter burners."

4. Your tendons, ligaments, joints, and bones have had the several weeks they need to become as strong as

your muscles will become after just a few days of exercise.

5. Your Fast Twitch type II muscle fibers have been converted to look and behave as much like Slow Twitch muscle fibers as possible.

6. Your flexibility, strength, and coordination will improve from the aerobic speed work.

7. You will learn the fine art of being patient as you learn how to endure longer and longer runs.

During Phase I, our main focus is on *endurance*. For veteran runners just cranking up for another season, this phase must be started a minimum of six to eight weeks prior to the racing season. For adults just making the transition from being a fitness jogger to a racer (which I call an Adult Onset Athlete), another four weeks is recommended.

Endurance is technically defined as the ability of your muscles to repeat a movement over and over again at a submaximal workload for a prolonged period of time. How prolonged? That depends on you. You can develop one mile's worth, or a marathon's worth of endurance—it's all a matter of proper training. When interpreting this definition to my runners, I like to say that *endurance* is the ability to finish the chosen distance, no matter how much you slow down before you are forced to walk.[4]

During this phase you should not exceed 75% to 80% effort, even on certain days I call Aerobic Speed days. I know that the term "aerobic speed" sounds like an oxymoron, but I'm talking about itty bitty bursts of speed for very short distances that don't take you over 80% effort. Although an 80% effort is borderline anaerobic, it's considered "easy" running in my system because not much lactic acid has a chance to build up. More about this in a moment.

The Easy Days

Three days a week (for example, Monday, Wednesday, and Friday), I want you jogging easily at a 65% to 75% effort only.

One day a week (usually Sunday) I want you to do a long run at only 60% to 75% effort. I recommend you enjoy the scenery and think about something relaxing. The distance covered should be no more than twice your average daily mileage. And on those other two days (i.e., Tuesday and Thursday), we'll do that aerobic speed work I talked about earlier.

The Hard Days

In Phase I, the "hard" days are not really so difficult, but they have that connotation because they are faster workouts. The speedwork, however, is devoted to the improvement of your biomechanics, not to the enhancement of your cardio-respiratory fitness.

Why do you need to do aerobic speed work?

Unfortunately, all the slow easy jogging has some undesirable side affects on your biomechanics. Your quads, hamstrings, calves and hip flexors tend to get weak and unbalanced and your quads, calves, hip flexors, adductors and hamstrings tend to get tight. To combat these poisonous side effects of slow running, you need an antidote of aerobic speed work.

But hold on. Don't worry: I'm talking about easy, gentle aerobic speed work here. I'm not talking about the killer intervals done at 90% effort during Phase III. We'll get there soon enough! These are user-friendly intervals capped at 80% effort. They're short easy runs of 50 meters, 100 meters, and 150 meters done strictly for your legs, not your lungs. To help you get a grip on this concept of "easy speedwork," here's a set of comparisons between aerobic and anaerobic intervals:

Here are some examples of Aerobic Speed Workouts that you could try on your hard days:

Aerobic Speed:

1. The most fun runners can have with clothes on.

2. Must be limited to no more than 20 seconds.

3. Is run with smooth, relaxed, fast strides.

4. Is over and done before a "first wind" blows.

5. Should cover between just 50 and 100 meters.

6. Absolutely hates lactic acid.

7. Is the featured workout of Phase I.

8. Can't be effectively measured on a heart monitor because it's over before the heart can catch up.

9. Doesn't need a long recovery jog, but take one anyway.

Anaerobic Speed:

1. Pain, Torture and Agony, even with clothes off.

2. Doesn't even start until you've run hard for at least 30 seconds.

3. You must be tight, tense and tying up.

4. Not effective once you reach a "second wind."

5. Probably is best endured over the last 100 meters of a fast 400M.

6. Teaches lactic acid tolerance.

7. Is the featured workout of Phase IV, The Peaking Period.

8. Should be timed on a stop watch because it's scary to see your heart rate so high on your monitor.

9. Essential that you take a complete "holiday" between repeats.

Aerobic Speed Workout 1

A. four laps of striding the straights, jogging the curves

B. four laps of 15/45 stop watch fartlek (i.e., stride for 15 seconds/jog for 45 seconds)

C. four laps of Heart Rate Fartlek (i.e., stride your HR up to 80%, jog it back down to 70%)

Strides are fast, but relaxed runs at a pace of least what you could run for one mile.

Aerobic Speed Workout 2

A. six laps of 150 meter accelerators (i.e., jog fast for 50 m, run easy for 50M, run fast for 50M, or, in other words, shift gears every 50M, noticeably increasing your speed but without going so hard that you exceed 80% by the end of the end of the 150M) with a 250M jog recovery after each acceleration

B. six laps of stride 50M/jog 100M

I promise that you'll love doing aerobic speedwork simply because you get to run fast and not get out of breath and tired doing it.

But what about Saturday? Isn't it one of the hard days? Well, yes. Saturday is the day you get to have some old-fashioned fun by going for a real run. Your target effort is 75-80% and should last for three to six miles, depending on your mileage needs for the week. Your pace should be about one minute per mile faster than your Sunday Long Run pace. However, let your heart be the guide by looking up the heart rate range in the chart of Appendix A. Later, your Saturdays will be switched over to racing or doing threshold runs. This is a transitional workout that will allow you to make the switch easier when you enter Phase II.

Look over the Training Pattern Sheet on pages 27-28. I've filled in the percentage effort blanks for a typical Phase I program. You would just have to fill in your own THR's and pace ranges by using Appendices A and B, respectively. You don't need to do it now, but at some point, please take the time to read the next section to learn the scientific rationale for Phase I workouts. Phase I sets the foundation for everything that follows and the easy runs will continue to play a very important role as recovery days from the harder workouts you'll have to do in the later phases.

Coach Benson's
Running, Ltd.

5600 Roswell Road Ste. 355 – Bldg. North
Atlanta, GA 30342
(404) 255-6234   Fax: (404) 255-0731

WEEKLY TRAINING PATTERN

Phase **I** during **9/7/92** to **11/1/92** for **FAVORITE PERSON**

I.   **EASY DAYS**

Mon , **Wed** , **Fri** , _____

These are slower runs for either building ENDURANCE &/or
RECOVERING from speed work and races. Relax and enjoy them.
Consider taking off one or two of these days off or, if you
must, jog easy for...

... **3** to **5** miles at **65** % to **75** % effort. Your THR will

be from _____ to_____ bpm at _____ to_____ min/mile pace.

After running, stretch the BIG 5 and run **4** to **5** strides

for **50** to **75** yards. These fast, but easy runs will help
to re-balance the biomechanics of your stride. LSD is bad
for you, if it's all you run.

II.   **HARD DAYS**

A.   **TUESDAYS**

These are fast workouts for building STAMINA &/or STRENGTH
or SPEED. First jog 1 to 2 miles, do the BIG 5 stretches,
and run 5 strides for 100 yards as a warmup. Then...
MILES OF AEROBIC INTERVALS

run **2** to **3** x **1** in_____ at **70** % to **80** % effort

with a **70%** jog recovery interval. Your THR will be _____

to_____ bpm at the end of each repeat, and should be down to

_____ bpm by the end of the interval of recovery jog.

Finish the workout with _____ sets of drills over _____ meters.
(The drills are hi knees, fanny flickers, skip bounding, and
toe walk.)

B.   **THURSDAYS**
                    Hilly

Run **1** to **3** miles of Heart Rate Fartlek at **70** % to

80 % effort. Your THR will be _____ to_____ bpm.

III.   STEADY STATE & ANAEROBIC THRESHOLD DAYS
                      S₄†ʊₙⒹₐ¥s

These workouts are exquisitely tailored to build up your STAMINA, without tearing you down the slightest bit. They are, in the immortal words of my HS biology teacher Mr. Fred Cook, anabolic, not catabolic. You can look it up....and while you're at it, note very well that these workouts are a from cry from real interval workouts, so don't worry if they seem easier than you're used to doing. Just enjoy not having to bust it for a change.

Start both of the below workouts with a mile or two of easy warmup running and then ...boogie on down.

A. If you are in Phase **I** or in marathon training,

run a total of **3** to **7** miles and include **1** to **5**

STEADY STATE miles at **70** to **80**% effort. Your THR will be

_____to_____bpm and your pace should be _____to_____mpm.

B. If you are in phases II, III, or IV, include

_____to_____ minutes of AT running at 80 to 85% effort.

Your THR will be _____to_____bpm and your pace will be

_____to_____mpm. Jog at least one mile to cool down.

IV.   LONG RUNS
                      SʊₙⒹₐ¥s

These workouts have two purposes: to build ENDURANCE during phase I and then to maintain it during the other phases. Thus, note well the changes in your THR when you switch phases.
Run easy from **3** to **7** miles at **60** to **75**% effort.

Your THR will be from _____to_____bpm and your pace will be

from _____to_____mpm.

    BE SURE TO STRETCH THE BIG FIVE REAL WELL AND RUN 4-5
    20 STEP STRIDES TO GET THE KINKS OUT AND TO RE-BALANCE
    YOUR PRIME MOVER RUNNING MUSCLES.
       Happy Trails -Coach Benson

The Science Behind Phase I Training

Although the list of adaptations at the beginning of this chapter should have given you a pretty good understanding of what's happening to you during Phase I, I believe it's important that you also know some of the more important bio-chemistry as well as a little more physiology.

Today, with the likes of infrared spectroscopy, chromatography, paramagnetic analysis, electron micrographs, and x-ray diffractometers, scientists can actually "see" the physical characteristics of some of the body's larger chemicals. This includes proteins and enzymes that play a major role in running. And most importantly, we know more about the role of glucose, ATP and those power houses in the running muscles called mitochondria. It's an intricate and complex system which far exceeds any mortal human imagination. Since you're going to be tinkering with the way your body derives its fuel, and you're going to be adjusting the body's ability to store those fuels, and you're going to mess around with your body's fuel delivery network, and since you're going to enhance its fuel processing system, you need to know about the chemical side of eating your veggies, carbo's and proteins. I've found that when my runners understand what a particular type of training is trying to accomplish in respect to the human body, they are less likely to make mistakes with their workouts. So you can look at the time invested in reading the next few paragraphs as time well spent. It may keep you from huffing and puffing when you could be cruising at a relaxed level of effort.

Adjusting Your Fuel Source

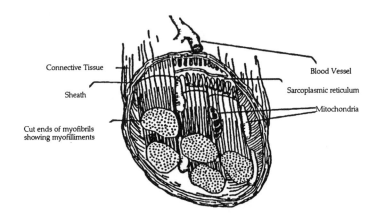

Connective Tissue

Sheath

Cut ends of myofibrils
showing myofilliments

Blood Vessel

Sarcoplasmic reticulum

Mitochondria

Enlarged Cutaway View of the Human Muscle

When we talk about *endurance* training in the context of 60% to 75% effort, we're talking about training that is going to adjust your fuel ratio of carbohydrate to fat. Both carbohydrate and fat are used to produce glucose for the ultimate catabolism into the real source of all muscle energy: ATP (adenosine triphosphate).

Comparing carbohydrates to fats as energy sources is like comparing kindling to logs for fire burning. It's a lot harder to burn the logs than the kindling. But once the logs start burning, they last a lot longer than the kindling. In other words, the fat is harder to burn. Fat is the better energy source. Again, to borrow a phrase from the author of *Fit or Fat*, Covert Bailey, "We want to become better butter burners." So how do we become better at burning this fat? You've got it—running long distances at that 60% to 75% effort! The reason you've got to run slow is because like those logs in the fireplace, you need lots of oxygen to keep the fatty flames burning. Aerobic running, means running with more oxygen. You may be saying to yourself about now, "I understand how this will cause me to burn a higher ratio of fat to carbohydrate during my long slow run, but how does the body make a more permanent adjustment?" The answer: Fats have aerobic enzymes associated with them that assist in the catabolism process. Long, slow distance running also increases these fat burning enzymes. It's part of the body's adaption process. This means that once you get your aerobic mileage up to a certain level, the body will burn more fat, *even in its resting state.*

Adjusting Your Ability to Store Fuel

As most of us know, the body doesn't have any trouble storing fat. However, it's not the same for storing carbohydrate. When carbohydrate is reduced to glucose, it will convert a certain amount into a slightly different chemical structure called "glycogen." What doesn't get stored or used immediately is converted into fat for long term storage.

Here's another benefit of Phase I training: Running at 60% to 75% effort will increase the amount of glycogen stored in the muscles. This means more kindling for the fire, and unless you're emaciated (less than 6% body fat) you already have plenty of logs. You need lots of kindling because, even though you have adjusted your fuel burning ratio, most of the energy needs for running still have to come from glycogen.

Although it's true some of this increased storage capacity is going to be more or less automatic from the increased enzyme activity that results from all this slow, easy running, the greatest gains in increased storage capacity for glycogen will come from the body's adaptation capabilities.

There are really three rules at work here:

1. Your body will adapt to gradual and progressive loads.

2. The body does not merely adapt, but actually overcompensates.

3. Adequate rest from heavy running must be allowed in order for the adaptation process to take place.

With respect to Rule No. 1, you are going to gradually be increasing your mileage during Phase I training. This increased mileage will be placing larger and larger demands on your glycogen stores.

Rules No. two and No. three say that your body will not only meet these demands, but given adequate time between the long runs, will overcompensate by storing more glycogen. This is why Phase I only allows the runner to take one long run per week—usually about twice the distance of his average daily mileage.

Each week must reflect a *gradual* buildup of mileage. The runner can't be jumping from a 20 mile week to a 40 mile week, for example. As you increase your average daily mileage, you are able to handle bigger, and bigger long runs on the weekends. How far you continue with this process is both a function of time and your target endurance level, i.e., mile, 5km, 10km, marathon, etc. However, if you increase this mileage too fast, the musculo-skeletal system will be one of the first parts of your body to let you know what it thinks of this folly. The Injury Fairy will tap you on your shoulder and next thing you'll know, you will have pulled a muscle. But not just your muscles are in danger of strains. Your other connective tissues (tendons, ligaments, joints, and bones) will also be at risk of over-use injuries.

These body parts aren't supplied with nearly the same number of blood vessels that reach the muscles. As a result of their poor circulation, they need much more time than the muscles to adapt to the stresses of exercise by getting as strong as the muscles. Have you ever heard that old chestnut: "Don't run too far or too fast too soon?" Well, you can bet that it wasn't made up by an out-of-work orthopedic surgeon or podiatrist.

Adjusting Your Fuel Delivery Network and Fuel Processing Capability

When you burn fuel in your car's carburetor, there's a carefully engineered adjustment of fuel and air. Car manufacturers often enhance this process by special fuel injectors, additional air intakes, and other goodies. It also helps performance if the car has a high octane gasoline being fed into it.

The human body's fuel delivery and processing system can also be enhanced. Through long, slow running, your blood becomes "high octane." That is, the blood will undergo an increase in myoglobin. Myoglobin provides larger stores of oxygen in the working cells for use when circulatory oxygen is inadequate. And you already know how important it is to have plenty of oxygen for the fuel burning process.

I wrote earlier of scientists' capability to see inside the runner's muscle cells. If you were to look in your leg's muscle cells, you would find some tiny egg-shaped organelles called mitochondria. These are often called the "power houses" of the muscle cells because they are the only place in which aerobic production of ATP can take place. The other system—the anaerobic production process of ATP (the one that causes that dreaded lactic acid)—happens in a fluid area outside these power houses. As runners, we want to delay using this other system as long as possible. Long, slow running will increase the number and size of these power houses so that you can do just that. With more factories for the aerobic production of ATP, you can handle the larger production demands of longer distances and larger workloads without relying too heavily on your anaerobic systems.

Closely related to this process is the increased ability, resulting from the long, easy running of Phase I, to supply blood to the muscle cells. The body accomplishes this by growing more capillaries to feed the muscle cells. This is an important issue since your blood carries the oxygen and is the medium by which the muscle cells cleanse themselves of unwanted chemical by-products, i.e., CO_2 and lactic acid. The larger the network of these capillaries, the more efficiently it can carry out this task.

Improving Your Heart and Lungs

It's a myth that runners have larger and stronger lungs. As a matter of fact, no study has even proved that training will improve a runner's overall pulmonary functioning. However, running does strengthen your diaphragm and rib cage muscles. This means that you can move more air through your system.

Another muscle, the heart, also is strengthened. Over time your heart will become larger and it will be able to move larger volumes of blood with fewer beats. This becomes most obvious for the runner when he takes his resting pulse. As you become fitter, your resting pulse slows. Some top athletes typically will have resting pulses between 35 BPM and 45 BPM. The untrained person will have a resting pulse usually in the 70's or higher. Something I like to show my runners is how lowering your resting pulse can lower your effort level required to handle a given workload. You can see this yourself by taking my heart rate/effort nomograph and drawing a series of lines from different resting pulses to your maximum heart rate.

Although Phase I training will have the largest effect on the heart and your resting pulse, all the phases of training will contribute to the heart's overall strength.

Improving Your Biomechanics

During Phase I training, you will be developing leg strength to the degree that the countless repetitions of one stride after another fatigues the working fibers and then causes new, fresh fibers to be recruited to help out.

Like weight lifting, there are two ways to build strength in the muscles: 1) light workload, but lots of repetitions, or 2) heavy workload, but few repetitions. We are using method one above during Phase I. Method two is reserved for speed and hill work. I'm sure you would prefer running further as opposed to running harder, so smile now. Enjoy Phase I.

How far should a person run during Phase I?

The answer to the above question depends on your training goals. Are you trying to get into shape for the mile, 5km, 10km, or marathon? Pick your poison. The table below categorizes runners as Rookie, Average Veterans, Above-Average and Elite. I have listed the recommended weekly mileage for each category.

Recommended Weekly Mileage				
	Mile	**5K**	**10K**	**Mar**
Rookie	15-25	20-30	25-35	50-60
Average Vets	25-40	30-45	35-50	60-80
Above Average	40-55	45-60	50-70	80-100
Elite	55-70	60-75	70-90	100-140

Normally, the *average runner* preparing to compete over distances from a mile to 10km, would want to work up to at least 25 miles per week minimum and around 45 miles per week maximum. Beginners might have to be happy with 12 to 15 miles per week. And an elite veteran runner may have to run as much as 60 to 70 miles per week in order to get that last ounce of improvement out of themselves.

Keep in mind that the mileage shown in the table from the previous page requires a gradual build-up. If you start experiencing sore knees or very tired legs, then, chances are that you are increasing your daily mileage too quickly. There is no exact science that I know of, for determining *how gradual* you make the mileage build-up. Certainly, you would never want to double your mileage from one week to the next. Generally, a 10% increase in weekly mileage could be handled fairly easily. And as another general rule, you would never want your long run to be more than twice that of your average daily mileage.

Putting it all together

Here is a summary of Phase I training:

Phase I Summary		
Purpose	**Adaptation Increases**	**Facts & Figures**
Aerobic conditioning to develop endurance, i.e., the capacity to reach the finish line without walking	1. Max O2 uptake 2. Efficiency of movement 3. Metabolism of fat 4. Connective tissue 5. Fast twitch II muscle recruitment	Mode: jogging Frequency: 6-7 times per week Intensity: 70-75% Duration: 20-90 min. Length of Phase: 6-12 weeks

To help you get used to seeing the correlations between heart rate and pace, check the Pace and Effort Chart on page 15 to see if your easy run pace at your selected target heart rates make sense when you see what type of race pace they predict. Remember that the common thread tying everything together is *common sense*. If your pace doesn't match with the predicted race times, go back and check your selection of THR's. It may mean that you're an exception with a far lower or higher Max HR than the average person.

Conclusion

Phase I is probably the most important phase of your training. The largest gains in oxygen power (VO2 Max) will come during this phase. You will be building a base upon which all the other phases of training must be supported. Without the physical and chemical gains of the body actually taking place by a proper and broad enough base training, you cannot hope to respond positively to the higher intensity training of the phases that follow. There are no short-cuts. You should never exceed the 70% to 75% effort level except for the short 80% effort aerobic speed workouts designed to keep the muscles loose and flexible. Your Saturday steady state run can also approach 80%, but keep the effort constant by slowing down the pace as you tire out near the end of the workout.

In the next chapter, we will continue building and maintaining this aerobic base, but we will move our focus to 80% to 85% effort workouts once or twice a week. These will be designed to delay the onslaught of lactic acid (the precursor of muscle lockup) during race conditions.

3. Phase II: Stamina

Here are the physical and mental adaptations you need to accomplish in this phase:

Your *stamina* will be developed when these bodily changes have taken place:

1. your maximum oxygen uptake will make another nice improvement as your capillary system greatly expands in response to the introduction of lactate threshold workouts.

2. your efficiency will continue to improve as your body learns how to decrease wasted movements. To be sure that your arms are not guilty of inducing rotary motion of your upper body, and also to be sure that you are not over-striding, it might be worth having the bio-mechanics of your stride analyzed by video taping.

3. your muscles will now start to learn how to deal with lactic acid.

4. you will start developing the "endurance" speed of your fast twitch muscle fibers as you carry a faster pace for longer distances.

5. your concentration will improve as the harder workouts encourage you to pay better attention to where and how you're going.

During Phase II, our main focus is on *stamina*. The ideal length of this phase is six weeks, but it could be shortened to just four weeks by veterans who have been through these phases before. Stamina is technically defined as the ability of your muscles to move your limbs through a specific range of motion at a given speed until that rate of turnover can't be maintained. When interpreting this definition to my runners, I like to say that stamina is the ability to get to the finish line without running "positive splits" (i.e., running slower and slower).

I often times refer to this phase of training as "Getting Ready to Race." The phrase is meant to create a little pre-season anxiety by including the dreaded word "race." During this phase, you should feel the urgent need to develop a higher level of conditioning whenever thoughts about upcoming races release a flock of butterflies in your stomach.

Stamina is best developed by adding anaerobic threshold (AT) workouts for four to six weeks before you race. Your anaerobic threshold is the physiological point at which your body stops using aerobic production of ATP as its primary source of energy (i.e., in the mitochondria); and instead switch over to its anaerobic system (i.e., in the fluid area outside the mitochondria) as its primary method for producing ATP. In plain vanilla talk, it's the edge of your "huff and puff" zone. It's a line that once crossed means rapid lactic acid accumulation. How rapid depends on how far over the line you go. With AT training we want to take you *right up to the line*, without venturing over it too much or too often.

I recommend two days a week of AT running at 80 to 85% of maximum effort as the cornerstone of this phase. Usually, an effort at this level requires a pace that's about 20 to 30 seconds per mile slower than your expected 10km race pace. These AT runs should last for

15 to 20 minutes. They can be run as three to four repeat miles or as uninterrupted "tempo" runs for the 15 to 20 minute duration. I suggest one or two of these AT workouts per week.

As you prepare for 5km and 10km racing, these are the workouts that help you develop a proper sense of race pace. If you're usually guilty of going out too fast, this slightly slower practice pace will give you a better feel for the effort you should maintain throughout a race.

What are the physiological benefits?

The intensity of AT runs is such that they are "comfortably hard." You are close enough to the upper threshold that you are beginning to accumulate some lactic acid, but you have not ventured past the threshold where a more rapid accumulation takes place. As you run at this pace, your body learns to deal with moderate levels of acidosis (acid pH shifts in the blood composite). You will also continue to increase capillarization to the muscles, as well as enzyme activity.

The AT runs are run faster and farther than the aerobic speed workouts you were doing several days a week during Phase I. By running faster a few days each week, your range of motion will increase as you "jump" farther with each stride. This longer stride will also increase flexibility in your legs and hips, and it will strengthen them, because more muscles are recruited to lift your body higher than in the slower Phase I runs.

When you run faster, you not only move forward, but you also raise your legs higher, so you're working harder against the pull of gravity (as with uphill running). You overload your muscles more quickly, but you also develop better coordination. Running miles and miles of slow distance is intended to fatigue (and thus condition) the muscle fibers, but faster running is meant to improve muscle strength and biomechanics.

Quite often I will have conversations with my runners as they are making the transition from Phase I to Phase II, and it usually goes something like this: "Hey Coach, we gotta talk. I jumped into a 5K this past weekend and could not hold race pace. My legs started tying up and I was really huffing and puffing after the first mile or so." This scenario is to be expected if you start racing before you have really had time for Phase II to take effect. This runner is experiencing a lack of stamina.

During Phase I, we were recruiting fewer muscle fibers and the intensity level of the training was low enough that we were not having to take our aerobic energy producing system to its upper limits. In contrast, as we raise the intensity level of training a few times per week in Phase II training, we will recruit more muscle fibers and test the upper limits of our aerobic system.

Returning to my example, this runner was probably putting out an effort, during the later stages of his first mile and a half, somewhere in the neighborhood of 90% to 92% effort. Unless he had incredible running economy, this put him well into the forbidden territory of Lactic Acid Land. Having this happen so early in a race is suicidal. A countdown clock had started ticking. That internal time bomb, known as muscle "rigor mortis," is set to go off. The runner can either slow down and make it to the finish line or ignore the signals of tiring legs and hyper-ventilation. If he chooses the latter course of action, he'll eventually start "locking up" way short of the finish line. Even worse, he could drop out lame with a pulled muscle.

In a way, I'm glad when a runner experiences this form of humility at the outset of Phase II. It illuminates the purpose of Phase II clearly. Whereas during Phase I we were working diligently on building up the runner's VO2 Max, like putting money in the bank, we're now going to help him spend his savings wisely. At the same time, we are protecting his hard earned savings by continuing to maintain the aerobic base.

How does Phase II training improve a runner's threshold point?

In well-trained athletes, the threshold point is usually reached at about 80% to 85% VO2 Max range. But keep in mind that we are just now getting into shape, which means your threshold point is not going to be that high. That's why when we start running at anything over 75% *effort* (in the 70% to 75% of VO2 Max range), we will experience some heavy huffing and puffing. Ideally, we would like to avoid that heavy huffing and puffing until we expend an effort in excess of 85%. In that manner, when racing the 5km at over 90% effort, you will not have ventured too far past the threshold point to lockup short of the finish line.

Threshold running is just one more way the body learns to adapt to specific workload. Since you are running close to a 10km race pace, you are teaching motor responses to more of the muscles actually used in racing than you were during Phase I. You are also beginning to deal with moderate levels of lactic acid.

These runs, particularly the type of "tempo" run that I recommend, help the body learn a "rhythmic" recruitment of muscle fibers and firing order of brain messages that get the body ready for racing.

The How, When, and Where of Phase II Training

The primary difference between Phases I and II is in the intensity of your workouts. The pattern stays the same: easy days on Monday, Wednesday, and Friday. In fact, they get easier because the work of building endurance is for the most part done. Now the objective is just to maintain your endurance. Your target zone of effort drops from 65-70% down to 60-65%. So look at the nomograph again in Appendix B and set your heart rate zone. That's the good news!

Now for the bad news: Tuesday and Saturday are harder! That's why those easy days must get easier— you need to replenish your glycogen supplies by working more aerobically, so it will be possible for your muscles to maintain that higher fat burning ratio you worked on during Phase I, and save a lot of that glycogen for your AT runs. This is important because the harder, slightly anaerobic workouts are going to require a much higher percent of glycogen as the major source of energy for the working muscles. Since the restoration process takes about one and one-half to two days of digesting carbos, you must work lightly on the intervening days.

On Tuesday, instead of those fun, little aerobic interval runs, you need to substitute long repeats of 800's, 1200's and miles. A sample workout would be:

1 x 800M at 85% effort with a jog interval until the heart rate equals 70% effort or lower
1 x 1200M at same criteria as above
1 x 1 mile at same criteria as above
1 x 1200M (same as above.)
jog 3/4 to 1 mile to warm down

Saturday's change will be a slight increase from 75-80% up to 85% for a run of 15 to 20 minutes. This is a true anaerobic threshold run in the finest sense of the name. Although you will find that it takes a very fast pace to get the effort up to the required 85%, the workout isn't a killer because it's over relatively soon. Furthermore, since the real secret is keeping the effort at exactly 85%, you will find yourself slowing the pace down more and more as the run progresses to the end. Of course, to be sophisticated enough to be able to do so requires that you constantly measure your working heart rate and since you probably can't do that and run too, you need to wear a good heart monitor. The remaining days of Phase II training stay the same as they were during Phase I. Thursday is still a day devoted to legs, not lungs. You go out and gambol around like a Spring colt as you stretch out your legs. Run some aerobic speed in bursts not lasting more than 20 or 30 seconds each. Avoid running hard or long enough to make yourself huff and puff. Stay aerobic and keep the workout moderate enough that you will be recovered by Saturday.

Your long run on Sunday also stays the same as it was during Phase I. Just get out there and grind out the mileage.

I have answered the How and When, now for the Where. Because of the "closeness" we are trying to establish with your anaerobic threshold, we need to have tight control over your heart rate. We can do this in part by watching the heart rate via a good heart monitor, but you will also need to have a constantly controlled workload. Hilly terrain will not work, because there is too much variability of workload. You must run on either flat streets or trails, or go to a track. Sorry. You can enjoy scenery on all the other days, but AT running takes total concentration and control.

Now take a look at that familiar pace chart on page 15 and take note of the Level of Effort column for Phase II training.

Putting It All Together

Here is a summary of Phase II training:

Phase II Summary		
Purpose	**Adaptation Increases**	**Facts & Figures**
Anaerobic conditioning, i.e., "getting ready to race," by developing stamina, the ability to maintain race pace.	1. Max O$_2$ uptake 2. Improve efficiency 3. Adapt to lactic acid 4. "Endurance speed" 5. Concentration	Mode: jog on easy days, run at anaerobic threshold (@20 sec/mile slower than race pace) Frequency: 2-3 times per week. Intensity: 70-85% Duration: 20-90 min. Length of Phase: 6-12 weeks

Conclusions

We're getting you ready to race with this phase of training. You're going to be able to do a decent job of holding race pace. However, you'll be chompin' at the bit for some speed work toward the end of this phase. You'll not be all that comfortable with the start of the race when everyone is semi-sprinting to establish pace and position. You may find it hard to handle surges. Downhill running may not feel that great either. Most of all, you're going to find in these early stages of making the transition into racing, a bit of discomfort in terms of how you are able to deal with the build-up of lactic acid. All this is why we have a Phase III of training. It will be your first real introduction into speed. We're going to teach your body how to deal with mean ol' lactic acid.

4. Phase III: Economy

Here's what your body and head will have to achieve in order to make you a better racer:

1. A final increase in your max oxygen uptake, especially because the workouts make you huff and puff hard enough to condition your respiratory muscles (the intercostal and diaphragm particularly) really well.

2. Another increase in the size of the capillary bed due to the sizable buildup of lactic acid you'll experience during your speed workouts.

3. Improved flexibility as your stride lengthens during the fast interval workouts.

4. Greater strength in the working muscles as the faster paces require that your legs push you further through the air, creating longer strides.

5. Better coordination between your mind, nerves and muscles as greater numbers of muscle fibers become involved.

6. Better concentration on the task at hand as your mind seeks the shortest path and quickest way to get these painful repeats over with.

7. Increased levels of human growth hormone contributed from the pituitary gland.

8. A probable decrease in libido due to the stress of heavy training

During Phase III, our main focus is on your *Economy*. This phase usually stretches out over the many weeks that make up just about all of one's season of competition. For high school and college runners, that usually means eight to 12 weeks. For road runners following a careful plan of assault on PR's and championships, this phase should be limited to only two to three months to avoid getting stale or peaking out prematurely. The combination of training fairly hard and racing frequently is a potent one and can flatten even the strongest runners in a hurry.

My applied definition of "economy" is: *the effort required to run a particular pace*. Thus, if you are an inefficient runner, owner of a stride that wastes lots of energy because of bad bio-mechanics, your economy would be bad because you would be making a greater than necessary effort to run. If you're a runner in lousy shape trying to run fast, your economy would be lousy because your undertrained muscle fibers would have to keep recruiting more and more additional fibers in order to sustain the pace that you're trying to keep. The higher the number of fibers involved, the greater the demands for energy and oxygen. This would be very uneconomical, and the spectacle you make of yourself isn't very pretty.

In the context of Phase III, I think of how many muscle fibers have to be recruited to train at faster than race pace. The greater the effort, the higher the number of muscle fibers that have to be recruited to move the limbs through a bigger range of motion at a faster rate. Just as car engines are built to deliver more RPM's at speeds way over the speed limit by using more and more of the available horsepower, training during Phase III is going to recruit more of your muscle power than you'll initially need when you slow back down to race pace.

For example, let's look at two runners at the same level of fitness. If both set out to run a 6:00 pace during a 10km race, economy may be the only difference between them. Both runners may have the same oxygen capacity (VO_2 Max), but Runner B is more frugal with his oxygen usage because she is more efficient (or as Coach Bob Sevene is fond of saying, "has better wheels"). After three and a half miles, Runner A's legs are beginning to tie up because she keeps recruiting more fibers to make up for her poor bio-mechanics. Runner B still has plenty of well-conditioned fibers left in reserve. Runner A is having to expend a lot more effort than Runner B and, all else being equal, will have to slow down sooner than her more economical rival.

The moral of the story is that distance runners cannot rely on their slow twitch (ST) fibers alone to carry this race pace load. We need to be able to recruit some of the fast twitch (FT) fibers to help out. Fiber recruitment and conditioning is "learned" through training. Phase III training will provide the right balance between ST and FT fiber recruitment to do the job most economically.

Another component of effort is the muscle fiber's ability to continue contracting in spite of high levels of lactic acid caused by insufficient oxygen during ATP production. This is exactly the situation during racing. Phase III training will bring improvement both psychologically and chemically. Psychologically, you will learn that no matter how bad you feel, you won't die, that you will recover and feel good again shortly after the run is over. Chemically, you will be improving your body's buffering capabilities—its ability to neutralize lactic acid. This will, in effect, give your muscle fibers more staying power at race pace.

How is this phase different from the previous phases?

If you are like most runners, you couldn't resist the temptation of racing during Phase II of your training. Phase II involved getting you used to running faster than Phase I, but you still weren't into the Big Leagues yet. Phase II was teaching your body to delay the on-slaught of lactic acid. Now comes the time to deal with reality. In races, you not only take your body up to threshold, you go beyond it. Phase III teaches your body how to cope with Lactic Acid Land.

Phase III begins the groundwork for developing speed. Working on your speed is simple, but not easy. Basically, you have to practice running faster in work-outs than you did in your last race. This will mean only a slight change in your training pattern because only your hard days (i.e., Tuesdays and Thursdays) will be different. The recovery days of Monday, Wednesday, and Friday should still be easy workouts of ambling along at 60-70% of maximum, basically as slowly as you can stand to go. Remember that the purpose here is to get your "leg energy" (your muscle glycogen) back and that it takes one and one-half to two days to allow that process to take place after a race (of 10km or less) or hard workout. These are the days, if you don't like to run seven days per week, to take off completely. Go for a walk or do some light cross training in the pool or on a bike, but take it easy.

Rest assured that *gold medals are usually lost on the recovery days!* This is when easy workouts degenerate into hard ones because of a macho disdain for appearing to wimp out in public. If you can't stand being mistaken for a jogger, then hiding inside on your easy days may be your wisest course to avoid overtraining. Your hard workout day of the week should now be Tuesday. This is your day for speed work, running intervals on the track.

It's probably time to offer a better definition for "interval." The word actually refers to the amount of *rest* you give yourself during some hard repetitive running. There are 1001 ways to do interval workouts and I could spend all day debating the relative merits of each. For now, let's keep things simple.

Take a look at our familiar Pace and Effort Chart on page 15. Direct your attention to the column designated for Phase III. This is the column that gives your 400M interval workout pace. By now, you should have a pretty accurate idea how fast you can run the mile, 5km or 10km. Use this information to determine your pace. Don't pick a time based on what you *want* to run. Use your current performance level.

Each "rep" that you do during this workout will be 400M long, that is, one lap around the track. You will do this at the pace indicated in the pace chart. After each fast lap, you will jog a very slow half lap to get your wind back. Keep in mind that the fast laps should feel like mini "races" because they are designed to duplicate the stress you feel during a race. However, since you're going to get to rest after each lap, you have to run a little faster than your race pace. You will notice that the paces are slower than you could do for one or even several all-out laps. That's a little bit of a problem, because there is a tendency to try to run each 400M faster than recommended in the chart. Don't!

If you are a veteran runner and notice that these fitness related paces are much slower than you've been used to in interval workouts, then you're on the brink of a great discovery: You've been doing the wrong kind of interval work. Hard work at this phase of training is *not* all-out work. These one lap runs should take only about 90% of your effort capacity. Surprisingly, that's all the effort it takes to keep you improving from race to race during your season. Harder, all-out workouts in which you tie up and "die" as you come down the last 100 yards are completely inappropriate. Don't kill yourself in practice. Save it for the races! That's the place to be a hero.

How many intervals should you do?

If this is your first time to attempt intervals, do between eight and 12. Some veterans can handle 16 to 18. Here is where your recovery heart rate becomes a big factor. You should be able to recover to a heart rate that corresponds to about 70% effort. When you slow jog that recovery 200 meters, if you find you can't recover to this heart rate, it's time to terminate the workout. You are either trying to do too many intervals or you are running too fast a pace. Don't try to gut it out.

You are going to be racing—perhaps a lot—during this phase, so your schedule needs to be flexible. On the week of a race, two miles worth of intervals is usually all that you can do and still recover by Saturday's race.

If you're not racing that week, then go ahead and run three miles of intervals and just be sure to take it very easy the next day.

As for the rest of the week, your other "hard" days are still Thursday and Saturday. Thursday you can include a mile or two (how much depends on whether or not you have a race on Saturday) of fartlek within your run for the day. Fartlek training is a Swedish system that features "speed play" involving changes of pace ranging from jogging to easy, short (10 to 20 second) "sprints." I put quotation marks around the word "sprint" to emphasize that these should not be full speed dashes that leave you gasping in deep oxygen debt. Just make them fast but smooth, relaxed runs that are a little faster than the pace you ran on Tuesday. As I like to say to my runners: "Think legs, not lungs."

Saturday is either a race day or an AT run day. If it's a day for the latter, during an easy run of several miles, include a segment of 15 to 20 minutes at the 85% AT effort level.

Now comes Sunday. This is still the same long run day. However, if you raced on Saturday, keep it no more than six or seven miles. It should be more of a recovery run (60-65% effort) than an endurance run. Don't worry. You won't lose your endurance as long as you're getting in a regular long run on the non-race weekends.

How Long Does this Phase Last?

Phase III will normally last eight to 12 weeks. By that time, you will be ready for the next phase of training.

Putting it all together

Below is a summary of Phase III training:

Phase III Summary		
Purpose	**Adaptation Increases**	**Facts & Figures**
The Aerobic Capacity or "competition season" phase to develop ECONOMY, i.e., the percentage of total number of muscle fibers recuited to hold race pace.	1. Max O2 uptake peaks 2. Capillary beds 3. Improved flexibility 4. Strength 5. Coordination 6. Concentration 7. Growth hormone 8. Reduced libido	Mode: jog on easy days, interval training on hard days. Frequency: 1 - 1 1/2 times per week Intensity: 90-95% Duration: 2-3 miles of repeats (i.e., 12 X 400M) Length of Phase: 8-16 weeks

Conclusions

During the final phase of training we will attempt to put the sharpest point on our "peak" as we can. We will make our greatest gains in establishing lactic acid tolerance and buffering ability. We will also make the greatest gains in establishing all the neuro-responses necessary for efficient FT fiber recruitment. The bottom line is: we're gonna get you as fast as possible! It's time to peak.

5. Phase IV: Speed

Remember that smart runners not only train intelligently, they know why they're doing each workout. Those who don't wind up paying me as their coach to do their thinking for them, and, like the chimp said when he climbed up into the counter and took a leak onto the cash register, "Folks, that will run into the money." I'm all for redistribution of the wealth (I charge a lot for coaching) but following the advice in this book can save you from having to seek expensive advice down the road.

The adaptations you seek in Phase IV are:

1. Improved lactic acid tolerance.
2. Increase in actual leg speed by maximizing your working muscle strength, by enhanced flexibility and by improved coordination. These factors may be summed up as "better biomechanics."
3. The ability to stay relaxed at ever faster racing speeds.
4. Greater economy from greater strength.
5. Return of lost libido.
6. Diminished appetite (helping you get down to your ideal body fat level).

Ultimately, your *speed* will improve, allowing you to come to a peak just in time for that most important race of the season. Depending upon how well you built your aerobic base during Phase I, you can plan to spend as little as two weeks and perhaps as many as several weeks in Phase IV.

Speed is generally defined as your ability to "sprint like hell," but I usually modify that to "the ability to run much faster than race pace and still be relaxed."

If you did Phase III properly, then you were not trying to see how fast you could run the 400 meters. Phase III was really more of an introduction to speed, during which I primarily wanted to ease you into learning to run fast. I was more interested in building your running economy. Yes, those intervals were fast—a lot faster than the threshold runs of Phase II. But they weren't (or shouldn't have been) all-out sprints.

In contrast, the intervals of Phase IV will be run at a 95% to 100% effort. You are going to have to depend more on your internal perceptions than the digital reading on your heart monitor to determine if you've reached a 95-100% effort . These repeats will be run for such short distances that your heart will not have time to catch up to your legs until the segment is over. Your heart monitor, at least those designed by Polar Electronics, averages heart rates. That is, it takes several internal readings and averages them before it outputs them to the liquid crystal display. This only further impairs your ability to get an accurate heart rate reading during very short interval runs. Furthermore, your legs will have run up an oxygen debt faster than Congress adds to our national deficit. Since you will probably reach the end of the repeat before your circulatory system can catch on to what happened to your legs, your heart rate may, in fact, peak *after* you stop running. Distances of up to 150 meters usually fit this category. Once you stretch it out to 200M and up to 400M, you may actually "tie up" enough from lactic acid accumulation that your turnover rate will drop off significantly. Once again your heart senses that you're slowing down and may drop below your maximum. In short, rely more on your stop watch and the training paces recommended in the right hand column of the Pace Chart.

Phase IV intervals are often referred to as *anaerobic overload intervals*. I strongly recommend that adult road runners concentrating on five and 10K 's never run longer than 30 seconds. Elite masters, 800 and 1500M, and younger runners competing in high school and college races will need to run up to 400M to get the full benefit of lactic acid tolerance training, but only a few very fast repeats need to be run to gain the benefits. Long rest intervals (up to 10 minutes) of recovery should be taken between repeats.

Start your workout by doing 4 x 150M at the pace shown on the pace chart for Phase IV. During this training session, I want you to purposely throw yourself into oxygen debt. Give yourself the usual jogging rest between each repeat of not more than one and one-half minutes. Four such repeats constitute a set. Between each set, there will be a recovery period. I usually have my runners jog at least 400 meters very slowly during this recovery period.

Now you are ready for the next set. This time, run six x 100M at the pace shown on the chart. Jog 200 meters rest between each repeat before stepping up to the line for the next 100 meters. Again, jog a 400 meter recovery following these six repeats.

Finally, I want you to run 8 x 50 meters at the suggested pace. Take a 150 meter rest in between each. Finish the session with a one mile warm down.

How About the Other Days?

During this phase, you have three days of rest and recovery or a light aerobic workout somewhere between 60% and 75% effort. These three days are alternated as before, and I suggest Monday, Wednesday, and Friday. Because the "hard days" of Phase IV are so tough, you're going to need these easy days to get those muscles reloaded with glycogen. In this same vein, it is important to put your Sunday (or whatever day of the week you take your long run) in the category of recreational running, shortening it down to eight miles maximum the week before a race.

Saturday will continue to be either a race day or an anaerobic threshold day. If it's an AT run day, continue to keep it no faster than the 85% effort of Phase II.

One day per week—I suggest Thursday—do three miles of "pickups." These should be relaxed speed surges of 15 to 30 seconds duration. If it is the week of a race, limit this pickup day to one or two miles of surges.

The Physiological/ Psychological Benefits

We are going to be improving your biomechanics by running full throttle. When you slow down to race pace, your legs will feel great. Submaximal paces will seem considerably easy to maintain. And this won't just be subjective perception! The prolonged periods of high lactic acid levels will improve your body's ability to deal with acid through its adaptive buffering capabilities. During Phase III the rest between repeats and the more moderate speed levels did not force your body to fully learn this science. Phase IV achieves this buffering capability more completely.

All muscle fibers have "tension generating" protein associated with them. During Phase IV training, a particular type of fast twitch fiber (FT Type IIa) increases its tension generating capability as another form of adaption. In plain ol' vanilla talk, these muscles become stronger. You will feel "bouncier"—a definite difference.

Your running economy will continue to improve. Not only will the muscles get stronger and able to do more work, you'll have more muscles firing because of improved neuromuscular recruitment.

Putting It All Together

The real key to proper peaking is taking a lot more rest between these high intensity workouts. A 60-year-old half miler I coached would cut down from his Phase I mileage peak of 120 miles per week to around 15 for the couple weeks before the World Veteran's Championships. Another of my 60-plus runners would cut back from his pattern of four days per week of running to just three workouts per week for his taper. Tapering off from the slow easy recovery runs to no running at all on recovery days is guaranteed to put the zippity back into your do-dah.

Below is a summary of the key points of Phase IV.

Phase IV Summary

Purpose	Adaptation Increases	Facts & Figures
The Aerobic Capacity or "peaking" phase to develop SPEED, i.e., the capacity to "sprint" and stay relaxed	1. Lactic acid tolerance peaks 2. Leg speed peaks 3. Relaxation at speed 4. Economy peaks 5. Return of libido 6. Diminished appetite	Mode: jog on easy days, sprinting and running at speeds 105-120% faster than Phase III Frequency: 1 per week Intensity: 90-100% Duration: 1-2 miles of repeats (i.e., 8 X 100M) Length of Phase: 2-4 weeks

6. Some Heart Rate Monitor Tips

Here are some general day-to-day helpful hints on using your heart monitor in training.

1. When warming up down, keep your heart rate as close to 60% as possible for at least five minutes.

2. To avoid the Dreaded First Wind, stay as close to 60% and absolutely do not exceed 70% of your max heart rate until you start sweating and are fully warmed-up, loose and ready to go to town.

3. To enjoy the Friendly Second Wind, gradually take your heart rate up from your warm-up zone to 75-80% MHR and hold it there just below your anaerobic threshold throughout your run. This effort zone is known as a "steady state run." It's everybody's favorite training pace and effort because it's bio-mechanically comfortable and yet still aerobic enough to allow conversation.

4. If you run primarily to control your weight, keep your HR in the 60-70% zone for the entire time in order to maximize your muscle's use of fat as its main fuel. Walk or Jog at least 6 or even 7 days per week for at least 45 to 60 minutes per day.

5. If you run primarily to keep your heart healthy, be sure to include two or three heart rate fartlek workouts per week. Just run your HR like a roller coaster up and down between 75 and 85% of MHR. This period of picking up and slowing down your speed should last

for 15 to 20 minutes per workout, not including warm-up and warm-down time.

6. If you run several times per week, you should follow a hard/easy pattern of training. Run hard by going longer or faster on one day. Recover by running shorter or slower on the next day. Fast running is in the 80-95% MHR zone. Slow runs are in the 60-75% zone. If you prefer to run comfortable, Steady State runs every day at a constant 75-80% effort, alternate between long and short runs.

7. If you run primarily to be fit and enjoy a good appearance, run with a friend who matches your fitness and ability. Run several times per week in the 60-70% MHR zone for 30-45 minutes per workout.

8. If your run primarily to have a strong, healthy heart and to be able to simply finish occasional five or 10K road races without getting so exhausted that you have to slow down to a crawl, you should push the Anaerobic Threshold of 85% for five minutes two or three times per workout a couple of times per week.

9. If you want to train to finish a marathon with a smile on your face, keep all of your mileage between 60-75% MHR, especially on your long runs.

10. Runs of 45 minutes and longer in warm weather may cause your THR to increase five to 10 BPM's as you become de-hydrated. This may happen without any apparent increase in your level of perceived exertion until your decreased blood volume causes a significant increase in HR and then a decrease in your cardiac output. At this point you'll notice how hard it suddenly has become to maintain your pace. Don't fight it—just slow down and keep your HR below 75%.

11. Your training HR may run 10-15 BPM higher than normal when you run in hot weather and your heart is recruited to run your radiator (cooling through sweating) system. Slow down if you reach 75% on easy days or you will turn your recovery workout into a Hard Day.

12. Paradoxically, you won't come near your actual Maximum Heart Rate by sprinting all out or running hard up a hill, unless you do so after 15 to 20 minutes of steady running. Initial bursts of speed just load your muscles with so much lactic acid that they fail before your heart reaches maximum. Hence the need for graded treadmill stress test, or a similar field test.

13. Paradoxically, your training heart rate won't always increase to match your perceived level of exertion. Sometimes your legs won't have recovered fully from the previous workout and you simply won't have the energy to run fast enough to elevate your HR to usual levels.

14. If you run competitively in 5K races, your HR should be between 85-90% by the end of the first mile and then go up slightly over the next two miles, hitting 95% plus at the finish.

15. If you run competitively in 10K races, your HR should be between 80-85% by the end of the first mile. Over the next three miles it will increase to 90-95% if you don't give in and slow down.

7. The True Middle Distances:

800 and 1500 Meters

Yes, I know that milers can't use the paces recommended in the Phase III column of the Pace Chart—at least if that's all the speed work they ran. But before we discuss how to adapt my charts to workouts for milers (and maybe even 800 meter runners, too) let me assure you that I appreciate the differences between these real middle distance events and their longer cousins the five and 10k. As a matter of fact, the half mile was my favorite event as a runner. My PR was 1:53.4 and my best race was a fifth place at the National AAU Jr. Championships back in 1963, results that weren't too bad for those days. Furthermore, some of my best coaching results have come with half milers, including a two-mile relay team that ran 7:21.3 indoors in the Astrodome in the early '70's. The half and the mile have special requirements because the folks who are willing to endure that much anaerobic discomfort to run them are special, or maybe a little crazy.

Training for the 800/1500/mile require more emphasis on speed work than we have included so far in our training patterns. Every discerning runner or coach has noticed by now that the speed of the 400's recommended in the phase III Economy column of the Pace

Chart doesn't seem fast enough. Well, they're right. Those paces won't develop the leg speed and lactic acid tolerance needed by runners who are going to run fast enough to spend at least 50% of their race in oxygen debt fighting off the effects of lactic acid buildup. So, obviously, what we need here are three separate, distinctive workouts each week with highly specific, different physiological and bio-mechanical objectives.

One of these workouts should be based on the paces recommended in the 90-95% Effort column. Since the exclusive purpose of this workout is to improve VO_2, longer repeats like 1200, 1000, 600 or even 400 meters are good distances to use. I like the repeats to total three miles, so it doesn't really matter if the workout is 3 x a mile or 12 x 400M. In fact, any combination of repeats (for example, 1 x mile, 2 x 800, 4 x 400) is fine for variety's sake. Keep in mind that this workout should mirror the fatigue response of a race with the heart rates not reaching upper target limits until the last 1/3 or 1/4 of the workout. Keep this in mind, too: runners don't have to kill themselves to increase their max oxygen uptake. *They should NOT be dying down the home stretch on each repeat.* Learning how to tolerate lactic acidosis is the objective of a different workout. Just run fast enough to reach 90-95% effort and your legs will love you for it.

Speaking of fighting off lactic acid build-up, that's the goal of workouts run at the paces recommended in the last column on the right of the pace chart. Those paces just happen to be calculated to be 120% faster than their counterparts to the left, but anything over 105% faster would be sufficient to put a miler into serious acidosis. To get to that stage of hurting is going to take repeats that last at least 30 seconds, but absolutely not longer than 75 seconds, as shown by research cited recently in Owen Anderson's *Running Research Newsletter*. The best distances would be 200 to 400 meters, with 300 probably the ideal, and from one to two miles total of repeats should be the limit of the workout. For example, 6 x 300M with a jog recovery of sufficient length to allow HR to return to at least 70% and then 6 x 200M with a similar recovery would be a good sample workout. The key is to do them at close to top speed and intensity. Longer repeats just allow the runner to slow down somewhat at the beginning in order to reach the finish without having to walk.

The third type training for milers should also be a separate and different workout. This one is for improvement of basic leg speed. Again the paces listed in the Phase IV Speed Column should be used to determine the speed of the workout for runners of different ability or different current levels of fitness.

Since the objective is simply to run "as fast as hell," the length of the repeat should obviously be kept very short. I have found that flying 50's and repeat 100's are ideal. The secret to these workouts is that the recovery period must border on "holiday length" because you want to be positive that all lactic acid causing oxygen debts have been repaid before you take off on another flyer. Keep in mind at all times that the objective of this workout is to work the legs, not the lungs. You want to develop leg speed while relying on the above workouts to develop the rest of your physiological capacities. Real speedwork is for development of your biomechanics: strength, flexibility and above all, coordination at top speed so that when you slow back down to race pace, you will feel relaxed and smooth, yet powerful.

Perhaps the best way to summarize a miler's approach is to review each training phase to see how his workouts would differ from 5K and 10K runners.

Phase I

No need to change anything here. The objective is to build up your aerobic capacity without losing your leg speed. The aerobic interval workouts will do that nicely, so just concentrate on getting in as much easy distance as you can in order to build your base as wide as possible.

Phase II

Again you can follow the basic pattern recommended in chapter 3. One small change would be to include six to eight 100M strides after Wednesday's workout just to maintain the leg speed you developed doing the aerobic intervals in Phase I.

Phase III

This would be the time to start following a Monday and Wednesday hard day training pattern in order to get in at least two of the three recommended workouts. You could rotate the three workouts over a three week period as follows: Week I: A & B; Week II: B & C; Week III: C & A. Since you're now in the middle of the competitive season, don't forget the conditioning value of the weekly races. Assuming that you're running in meets on Saturdays, you're getting three butt busters per week. Rest assured that you won't get out of shape on that kind of diet. You should, however, run eight to 10 x 100M strides after each easy distance run on your recovery days.

Phase IV

To come to a championship or PR peak, forget about your Max Oxygen Uptake type workouts at 90-95% effort. And forget about your endurance maintenance workouts of 60-70% effort. Taper your mileage down by taking more days per week completely off or by just going to the track and jogging a few miles to warmup for a short series of easy 50 to 75m strides on the grass. The other two workouts of the week should be Lactic Acid Tolerance repeats of 400M to 500M at top speed. Ideally you would do 2-4 x 400M with several minutes rest in between to totally recover. Try to run them at the pace indicated in the Speed Column of the Pace Chart. The second "hard" workout would be the leg speed workout of 50 to 100 sprints. An example would be 6-8 x 100M with a 300M jog between each one. Remember that a major component of speed is strength and that strength can be broken down into two components: 1) muscle fibers that have been conditioned through overload to become stronger and better able to lift you off the ground, and 2) muscle groups that have been totally replenished with supplies of glycogen, the rocket fuel needed to supply anaerobic effort.

Summary

We tend to overlook one training factor that can have a great impact on our racing readiness: consistency. All it really takes to perform up to our potential is following a training program that offers *frequent* workouts at a *moderate* effort on a *consistent* basis.

As John Parker puts it in *Once a Runner*, his great novel about running, "There are no secrets." So, as our favorite shoe company so succinctly puts it, "Just do it."

I hope this guide helps you achieve your running goals.

Notes

[1]This particular nomograph is a state-of-the-art "work of art" designed with help from my friends Ned Frederick, Ph.D. Exercise Physiologist and mathematician Larry Simpson, two exercise experts of the first order. They agree that calculating THR's is an extremely critical and highly necessary chore to train smart.

[2]The Finnish physiologist M.J. Karvonen gets credit for recognizing the importance of including RHR's when calculating THR's. This is why RHR is shown on the left hand axis.

[3]We are using the formula published by A. Hamid Hakki, et al, reported in the July '83 issue of *Cardiovascular Reviews and Reports*. Dr. Hakki is a medical doctor at the William Likoff Cardiovascular Institute in Philadelphia. His research, and similar efforts by Luger, et al, in Canada, has led to this formula, which is more accurate for predicting the maximum heart rate of chronically fit people like athletes.

[4]Some coaches, physiologists, and authors include in their definition of endurance: "aerobic endurance" used interchangeably with the word "stamina" and "anaerobic endurance" used interchangeably with the words "speed endurance." I do not use the word "endurance" to describe stamina or speed training. This is my personal preference. It stems mainly from the fact that I want my runners to equate easy running with endurance training. I don't want semantical differences with other coaches or systems getting them confused.

[5]For years I have struggled to find a name for this phase of training. I wanted this word to be a cousin of the familiar terms used by exercise specialists to describe the different components of physical fitness. Words like "endurance," "stamina," and "speed" are understood by most people to be the by-products of being in shape. Once their applied definition is offered, most runners quickly understand their usage in the context of our sport.

Initially, I labeled this period the "Speed" Phase because it involved training at faster than race pace, and that happened to be my applied definition of the word "speed." But that was also a good title for Phase IV because workouts featured in that phase involved some really fast running. So much, in fact, that it eventually became apparent to me that "speed" was really better used to name Phase IV. So off I went searching for a new name for my little orphan Phase III.

Coach Jack Daniels, Ph.D., Cortland State University, has defined "running economy" as the amount of oxygen required for any individual to maintain any particular submaximal running pace. Tim Noakes, MD, (*The Lore of Running*) and Dave Martin, Ph.D., Georgia State University, (*Training Distance Runners*) both refer to "economy" as the thriftiness by which one uses oxygen during running. The more I read by these giants in our field, the more I liked the ring that the word "economy" had to it. It was a familiar word, and one loaded with analogy potential. Since I love to draw comparisons between our exercising bodies and a car's engine, fuel system and transmission, I began to look at the bio-mechanical as well as the physiological implications that using "economy" to describe Phase III offered me.

Acknowledgements

As a coach I probably make a better teacher. Scratch my tanned coach's hide and I'm sure that underneath you'd find a frustrated professor. In fact, it's as important to me that my runners know why they're doing a workout as it is that they do it swiftly. This book represents my modest contribution to the ever-increasing body of Coachly Wisdom.

But before you say, "Thanks, Coach," it is only fitting that I acknowledge those who have made this manual possible. Most importantly I wish to thank my friend Larry Simpson who first came to me to become a more competitive masters runner. Larry is a math whiz and part-time physiologist who has applied for a patent for a dedicated computer that uses a mathematical model to replace a human coach. I say this with tongue in cheek because we know that no dumb computer could ever replace a real coach, especially one as good looking as me. Still, Mom didn't raise any idiots; I decided to keep a close eye on him.

Since much of the material came from articles I have written for several running and fitness publications, a huge amount of editing was required in order to make everything flow together. Larry's job was to help organize my original material into something coherent and help pare it down into a simple little workbook that would concentrate solely on the design of workouts.

I would also like to thank Owen Anderson, Ph.D. (editor and publisher of *Running Research News*) who provided invaluable technical assistance. Owen critiqued the entire first draft that we issued at my camps last summer and helped me get my physiological facts lined up in the right order for this public edition. Also, thanks to another physiologist of the First Order, Ned Fredericks, Ph.D. (Exeter Research) who provided me with my first chart relating percentage of effort to heart rate. Later, he and Larry Simpson worked together on their computers to expand and improve the chart. Thanks also to Dave Martin, M.D., Ph.D. (Georgia State University). I have Doctor Dave's research and friendship to thank for providing data that validated what I had figured out through years of coaching—optimized running performances requires four different phases of training. And I don't want to forget fellow coach Jack Daniels, Ph.D. (Cortland State University). Most of Larry's data used to generate the pace charts were mathematically modeled from the data reported in technical articles written by Jack. This same data was used by Amby Burfoot in an article he wrote for *Runner's World* several years ago, entitled, "The Perfect Pace." Amby was one of the first to publish Jack Daniel's training pace table based on current 10km performance. Larry and I have expanded on their great work and, hopefully, by refining and adding, have improved it.

My modest contribution has been to link *pace* with *target heart rates* and tie this all together into the philosophy for individualizing training that I call *Effort Based Training* (EBT). Thanks also to all the many other coaches, runners and friends who have supported my efforts over the years.

I especially want to thank my wife and friend, Betty, for being "the wind beneath my wings." Only with her loyalty and tireless support has any of my work been possible.

About the Author

Roy T. Benson, MPE, C.F.I., is an exercise physiologist and coach. He has a Master's Degree in physical education with emphasis in exercise physiology, from the University of Florida. He also holds a B.A. degree from Dartmouth College. He has worked as a specialist in adult physical fitness since 1976, and holds a national certification as Fitness Instructor from the American College of Sports Medicine. He has presented over 300 professional papers and lectures for academic and popular audiences. Currently, he is contributing editor for *Atlanta Health and Fitness Magazine, Running Journal* and *Running Times* magazines.

He was co-founder and co-owner of Fitness, Inc. in 1976, the first hospital-based fitness, rehabilitation, and health promotion program in the state of Florida. He also founded and directed the Wellness Center at North Florida Regional Hospital in Gainesville, one of the nation's first such hospital centers. This program and its sister cardiac rehab and back rehab programs, served as the model for other HCA (Hospital Corp. of America) hospitals.

He has been a competitive runner for 37 years, with personal bests of 1:53.4 for 880 yds, and 4:19.8 for the mile. As a master's competitor, he has run 36:06 for the 1OK, 17:22 for the 5K, 4:52 for the mile, and 3:09:05 for the marathon.

His coaching experience includes 31 years as a professional track and distance running coach. The combined records of his military, high school, university, and club teams exceed an .800 winning percentage. During his ten years of coaching at the University of Florida (which included six years as the head cross country coach, and three years as the head track and field coach), the Gators won two SEC track championships, developed numerous NCAA All-Americans and boasted two NCAA individual champions.

He served as the first president and later as the executive director of the world-famous Florida Track Club that placed gold medal marathon winner Frank Shorter, along with Jack Bacheler, Jeff Galloway, and Ron Jourdan on the 1972 U.S. Olympic team. Shorter and silver medalist pole vaulter Dave Roberts repeated on the 1976 Olympic team. Benson also served as the national advisory coach for the 1972 Philippine Olympic team at the Munich Olympics.

Currently Benson is the owner and president of Running, Ltd., a company that operates a national series of running camps, offers private coaching services to adult runners, and writes exercise prescriptions for physicians' patients.

Appendix

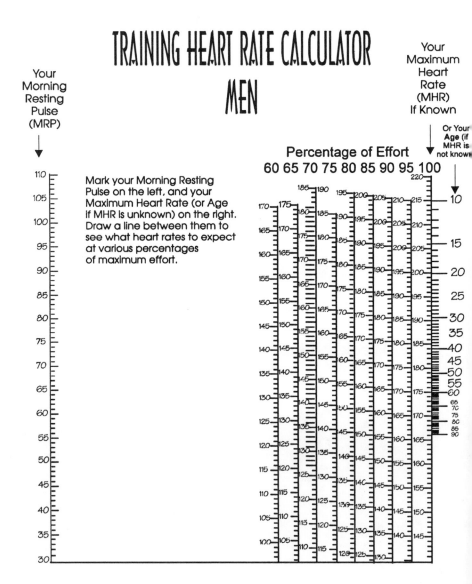

TRAINING HEART RATE CALCULATOR
MEN

Your Morning Resting Pulse (MRP)

Your Maximum Heart Rate (MHR) If Known

Or Your Age (if MHR is not known)

Percentage of Effort
60 65 70 75 80 85 90 95 100

Mark your Morning Resting Pulse on the left, and your Maximum Heart Rate (or Age if MHR is unknown) on the right. Draw a line between them to see what heart rates to expect at various percentages of maximum effort.

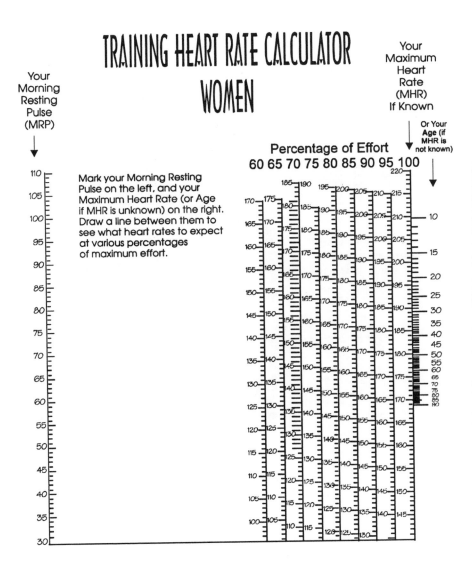

Pace & Effort Chart
For Four Phases of Training

			Percentages of Maximum Heart Rate -->	60 to 65%	70 to 75%	80 to 85%	90 to 95%	95 to 100%
If your current mile time is:	Or your current 5K time is:		Or if current 10K time is:	Your Recovery Pace will be: (mile)	Your Phase I Pace will be: (mile)	Your Ph. II Pace will be: (mile)	Your Ph. III Pace will be: (440M)	Your Phase IV Pace will be: (100M)
03:45	13:00 (04:11/mi)		27:00 (04:21/mi)	05:51	05:30	04:42	01:01.9	00:13.0
03:54	13:29 (04:21/mi)		28:00 (04:30/mi)	06:03	05:42	04:52	01:04.1	00:13.4
04:02	13:58 (04:30/mi)		29:00 (04:41/mi)	06:15	05:53	05:02	01:06.2	00:13.8
04:11	14:27 (04:39/mi)		30:00 (04:50/mi)	06:27	06:05	05:11	01:08.3	00:14.2
04:20	14:56 (04:49/mi)		31:00 (05:00/mi)	06:40	06:16	05:21	01:10.5	00:14.6
04:28	15:25 (04:58/mi)		32:00 (05:10/mi)	06:52	06:28	05:31	01:12.6	00:15.1
04:37	15:54 (05:07/mi)		33:00 (05:19/mi)	07:04	06:39	05:41	01:14.8	00:15.6
04:46	16:23 (05:18/mi)		34:00 (05:29/mi)	07:16	06:51	05:51	01:16.9	00:16.0
04:54	16:52 (05:26/mi)		35:00 (05:39/mi)	07:28	07:02	06:00	01:19.1	00:16.5
05:03	17:21 (05:35/mi)		36:00 (05:49/mi)	07:40	07:14	06:10	01:21.2	00:16.9
05:12	17:49 (05:45/mi)		37:00 (05:58/mi)	07:52	07:25	06:20	01:23.3	00:17.4
05:21	18:18 (05:54/mi)		38:00 (06:08/mi)	08:04	07:36	06:30	01:25.5	00:17.8
05:29	18:47 (06:03/mi)		39:00 (06:17/mi)	08:16	07:48	06:39	01:27.6	00:18.3
05:38	19:16 (06:13/mi)		40:00 (06:27/mi)	08:28	07:59	06:49	01:29.7	00:18.7
05:47	19:45 (06:22/mi)		41:00 (06:37/mi)	08:40	08:10	06:59	01:31.8	00:19.1
05:56	20:14 (06:31/mi)		42:00 (06:46/mi)	08:52	08:21	07:09	01:33.9	00:19.6
06:04	20:43 (06:41/mi)		43:00 (06:56/mi)	09:03	08:32	07:18	01:36.1	00:20.0
06:13	21:11 (06:50/mi)		44:00 (07:06/mi)	09:15	08:43	07:28	01:38.2	00:20.5
06:22	21:41 (06:59/mi)		45:00 (07:16/mi)	09:27	08:54	07:37	01:40.3	00:20.9
06:31	22:10 (07:09/mi)		46:00 (07:25/mi)	09:38	09:05	07:47	01:42.5	00:21.4
06:39	22:38 (07:18/mi)		47:00 (07:35/mi)	09:50	09:16	07:56	01:44.6	00:21.8
06:48	23:07 (07:27/mi)		48:00 (07:44/mi)	10:01	09:27	08:06	01:46.7	00:22.2
06:57	23:36 (07:37/mi)		49:00 (07:54/mi)	10:13	09:38	08:15	01:48.8	00:22.6
07:06	24:05 (07:46/mi)		50:00 (08:04/mi)	10:24	09:49	08:25	01:50.9	00:23.1
07:15	24:34 (07:55/mi)		51:00 (08:14/mi)	10:35	10:00	08:34	01:52.9	00:23.5
07:23	25:03 (08:05/mi)		52:00 (08:23/mi)	10:46	10:10	08:44	01:55.0	00:24.0
07:32	25:32 (08:14/mi)		53:00 (08:33/mi)	10:58	10:21	08:53	01:57.1	00:24.4
07:41	26:01 (08:24/mi)		54:00 (08:43/mi)	11:09	10:32	09:02	01:59.1	00:24.8
07:50	26:30 (08:33/mi)		55:00 (08:52/mi)	11:20	10:42	09:12	02:02.4	00:25.5
07:59	26:59 (08:42/mi)		56:00 (09:02/mi)	11:31	10:53	09:21	02:03.3	00:25.7
08:07	27:28 (08:51/mi)		57:00 (09:11/mi)	11:42	11:03	09:30	02:05.3	00:26.1
08:16	27:56 (09:01/mi)		58:00 (09:21/mi)	11:52	11:13	09:39	02:07.4	00:26.5
08:25	28:25 (09:10/mi)		59:00 (09:31/mi)	12:03	11:24	09:48	02:09.4	00:27.0
08:34	28:54 (09:19/mi)		60:00 (09:41/mi)	12:14	11:34	09:57	02:11.4	00:27.4

Compiled by: **Larry Simpson**
References: Separately published research of J. Daniels & M. J. Karvonen; also Amby Burfoot, ``The Perfect Pace,'' *Runner's World*

Coach Benson's
Running, Ltd.

5600 Roswell Road Ste. 355 - Bldg. North
Atlanta, GA 30342
(404) 255-6234   Fax: (404) 255-0731

Training Plan And Race Schedule

WK OF DATE	PHASES	M/WK	DAY/WK	SATURDAY	Sun/LR

Coach Benson's
Running, Ltd.

5600 Roswell Road Ste. 355 - Bldg. North
Atlanta, GA 30342
(404) 255-6234   Fax: (404) 255-0731

Training Plan And Race Schedule

WK OF DATE	PHASES	M/WK	DAY/WK	SATURDAY	Sun/LR

Coach Benson's
Running, Ltd.

5600 Roswell Road Ste. 355 - Bldg. North
Atlanta, GA 30342
(404) 255-6234   Fax: (404) 255-0731

Training Plan And Race Schedule

WK OF DATE	PHASES	M/WK	DAY/WK	SATURDAY	Sun/LR

Coach Benson's
Running, Ltd.

5600 Roswell Road Ste. 355 – Bldg. North
Atlanta, GA 30342
(404) 255-6234   Fax: (404) 255-0731

Training Plan And Race Schedule

WK OF DATE	PHASES	M/WK	DAY/WK	SATURDAY	Sun/LR

Coach Benson's
Running, Ltd.

5600 Roswell Road Ste. 355 - Bldg. North
Atlanta, GA 30342
(404) 255-6234   Fax: (404) 255-0731

Training Plan And Race Schedule

WK OF DATE	PHASES	M/WK	DAY/WK	SATURDAY	Sun/LR

Coach Benson's
Running, Ltd.

5600 Roswell Road Ste. 355 – Bldg. North
Atlanta, GA 30342
(404) 255-6234   Fax: (404) 255-0731

Training Plan And Race Schedule

WK OF DATE	PHASES	M/WK	DAY/WK	SATURDAY	Sun/LR

Coach Benson's
Running, Ltd.

5600 Roswell Road Ste. 355 – Bldg. North
Atlanta, GA 30342
(404) 255-6234   Fax: (404) 255-0731

WEEKLY TRAINING PATTERN

Phase ____ during _____ to _____ for _____

I.   **EASY DAYS**

_____,_____,_____,_____

These are slower runs for either building ENDURANCE &/or
RECOVERING from speed work and races. Relax and enjoy them.
Consider taking off one or two of these days off or, if you
must, jog easy for....

...____to___miles at ____% to____% effort. Your THR will

be from____to____bpm at_____to_____min/mile pace.

After running, stretch the BIG 5 and run ____to____strides

for ____to____yards. These fast, but easy runs will help
to re-balance the biomechanics of your stride. LSD is bad
for you, if it's all you run.

II.   HARD DAYS

A.   _____

These are fast workouts for building STAMINA &/or STRENGTH
or SPEED. First jog 1 to 2 miles, do the BIG 5 stretches,
and run 5 strides for 100 yards as a warmup. Then...

run____to____X _____in_____at____%to____% effort with

a_____jog recovery interval. Your THR will be_____to_____

bpm at the end of each repeat, and should be down to

_____bpm by the end of the interval of recovery jog.

Finish the workout with ____ sets of drills over ____meters.
(The drills are hi knees, fanny flickers, skip bounding, and
toe walk.)

B.   _____

Run ____to____miles of Heart Rate Fartlek at _____% to_____%

effort. Your THR will be _____to_____bpm.

III.   STEADY STATE & ANAEROBIC THRESHOLD DAYS

   These workouts are exquisitely tailored to build up your
STAMINA, without tearing you down the slightest bit. They
are, in the immortal words of my HS biology teacher Mr.
Fred Cook, anabolic, not catabolic. You can look it
up....and while you're at it, note very well that these
workouts are a from cry from real interval workouts, so
don't worry if they seem easier than you're used to doing.
Just enjoy not having to bust it for a change.

             Start both of the below workouts with a mile or
two of easy warmup running and then ...boogie on down.

      A. If you are in Phase I or in marathon training,

run a total of _____to_____STEADY STATE miles and include
_____to_____miles at _____to____% effort. Your THR will be

_____to_____bpm and your pace should be _____to_____mpm.

      B. If you are in phases II, III, or IV,

include _____to_____minutes of AT running at 80 to 85%

effort. Your THR will be_____to_____bpm and your pace wil

be_____to_____mpm. Jog at least one mile to cool down.

IV.   LONG RUNS

These workouts have two purposes: to build ENDURANCE during
phase I and then to maintain it during the other phases.
Thus, note well the changes in your THR when you switch
phases.
Run easy from _____to_____miles at _____to_____% effort.

Your THR will be from_____to_____bpm and your pace will be

from _____to _____mpm.

      BE SURE TO STRETCH THE BIG FIVE REAL WELL AND RUN 4-5
      20 STEP STRIDES TO GET THE KINKS OUT AND TO RE-BALANCE
      YOUR PRIME MOVER RUNNING MUSCLES.
             Happy Trails -Coach Benson

Coach Benson's
Running, Ltd.

5600 Roswell Road Ste. 355 – Bldg. North
Atlanta, GA 30342
(404) 255-6234   Fax: (404) 255-0731

WEEKLY TRAINING PATTERN

Phase _____ during _____ to _____ for _____

I.   <u>EASY DAYS</u>

_____,_____,_____,_____

These are slower runs for either building ENDURANCE &/or
RECOVERING from speed work and races. Relax and enjoy them.
Consider taking off one or two of these days off or, if you
must, jog easy for....

...____to ___miles at ____% to___% effort. Your THR will

be from____to____bpm at____to____min/mile pace.

After running, stretch the BIG 5 and run ____to____strides

for ____to___yards. These fast, but easy runs will help
to re-balance the biomechanics of your stride. LSD is bad
for you, if it's all you run.

II.   <u>HARD DAYS</u>

     A.   _____

These are fast workouts for building STAMINA &/or STRENGTH
or SPEED. First jog 1 to 2 miles, do the BIG 5 stretches,
and run 5 strides for 100 yards as a warmup. Then...

run____to____X _____in_____at____%to____% effort with

a_____jog recovery interval. Your THR will be____to_____

bpm at the end of each repeat, and should be down to

_____bpm by the end of the interval of recovery jog.

Finish the workout with ____ sets of drills over ___meters.
(The drills are hi knees, fanny flickers, skip bounding, and
toe walk.)

     B.   _____

Run ____to____miles of Heart Rate Fartlek at _____% to_____%

effort. Your THR will be _____to_____bpm.

III.   <u>STEADY STATE & ANAEROBIC THRESHOLD DAYS</u>

    These workouts are exquisitely tailored to build up your
STAMINA, without tearing you down the slightest bit. They
are, in the immortal words of my HS biology teacher Mr.
Fred Cook, anabolic, not catabolic. You can look it
up....and while you're at it, note very well that these
workouts are a from cry from real interval workouts, so
don't worry if they seem easier than you're used to doing.
Just enjoy not having to bust it for a change.

            Start both of the below workouts with a mile or
two of easy warmup running and then ...boogie on down.

    A. If you are in Phase I or in marathon training,

run a total of _____to_____STEADY STATE miles and include
_____to_____miles at _____to____% effort. Your THR will be

_____to_____bpm and your pace should be _____to_____mpm.

    B. If you are in phases II, III, or IV,

include _____to_____minutes of AT running at 80 to 85%

effort. Your THR will be_____to_____bpm and your pace wil

be_____to_____mpm. Jog at least one mile to cool down.

IV.   <u>LONG RUNS</u>

These workouts have two purposes: to build ENDURANCE during
phase I and then to maintain it during the other phases.
Thus, note well the changes in your THR when you switch
phases.
Run easy from _____to_____miles at _____to_____% effort.

Your THR will be from_____to_____bpm and your pace will be

from _____to _____mpm.

        BE SURE TO STRETCH THE BIG FIVE REAL WELL AND RUN 4-5
        20 STEP STRIDES TO GET THE KINKS OUT AND TO RE-BALANCE
        YOUR PRIME MOVER RUNNING MUSCLES.
              Happy Trails -Coach Benson

Coach Benson's
Running, Ltd.

5600 Roswell Road Ste. 355 – Bldg. North
Atlanta, GA 30342
(404) 255-6234   Fax: (404) 255-0731

WEEKLY TRAINING PATTERN

Phase _____ during _____ to _____ for _____

I.   <u>EASY DAYS</u>

_____,_____,_____,_____

These are slower runs for either building ENDURANCE &/or
RECOVERING from speed work and races. Relax and enjoy them.
Consider taking off one or two of these days off or, if you
must, jog easy for....

...____to___miles at ____% to___% effort. Your THR will

be from____to____bpm at____to____min/mile pace.

After running, stretch the BIG 5 and run ____to____strides

for ____to____yards. These fast, but easy runs will help
to re-balance the biomechanics of your stride. LSD is bad
for you, if it's all you run.

II.   <u>HARD DAYS</u>

    A.   _____

These are fast workouts for building STAMINA &/or STRENGTH
or SPEED. First jog 1 to 2 miles, do the BIG 5 stretches,
and run 5 strides for 100 yards as a warmup. Then...

run____to____X _____in_____at____%to____% effort with

a_____jog recovery interval. Your THR will be_____to_____

bpm at the end of each repeat, and should be down to

_____bpm by the end of the interval of recovery jog.

Finish the workout with ____ sets of drills over ____meters.
(The drills are hi knees, fanny flickers, skip bounding, and
toe walk.)

    B.   _____

Run ____to____miles of Heart Rate Fartlek at _____% to_____%

effort. Your THR will be _____to_____bpm.

III.   **STEADY STATE & ANAEROBIC THRESHOLD DAYS**

These workouts are exquisitely tailored to build up your STAMINA, without tearing you down the slightest bit. They are, in the immortal words of my HS biology teacher Mr. Fred Cook, anabolic, not catabolic. You can look it up....and while you're at it, note very well that these workouts are a from cry from real interval workouts, so don't worry if they seem easier than you're used to doing. Just enjoy not having to bust it for a change.

Start both of the below workouts with a mile or two of easy warmup running and then ...boogie on down.

A. If you are in Phase I or in marathon training,

run a total of _____ to _____ STEADY STATE miles and include _____ to _____ miles at _____ to _____ % effort. Your THR will be

_____ to _____ bpm and your pace should be _____ to _____ mpm.

B. If you are in phases II, III, or IV,

include _____ to _____ minutes of AT running at 80 to 85%

effort. Your THR will be _____ to _____ bpm and your pace wil

be _____ to _____ mpm. Jog at least one mile to cool down.

IV.   **LONG RUNS**

These workouts have two purposes: to build ENDURANCE during phase I and then to maintain it during the other phases. Thus, note well the changes in your THR when you switch phases.
Run easy from _____ to _____ miles at _____ to _____ % effort.

Your THR will be from _____ to _____ bpm and your pace will be

from _____ to _____ mpm.

BE SURE TO STRETCH THE BIG FIVE REAL WELL AND RUN 4-5 20 STEP STRIDES TO GET THE KINKS OUT AND TO RE-BALANCE YOUR PRIME MOVER RUNNING MUSCLES.
Happy Trails -Coach Benson

A Quick, Easy, and Inexpensive Way to Get into Heart Monitor Training . . .

HEART Monitor Training
for the Compleat Idiot
John L. Parker, Jr.

This great technology has finally become user-friendly and reliable enough for us to recommend these particular products as an invaluable tools for the athlete in serious training.

In my opinion, the Polar Favor and the Polar Edge represent milestones in this technology.

The No-Brainer Solution

The Favor has no buttons to push, nothing to set, no beeps, chimes, or little computer voices. It doesn't even have an on-off switch. When you hold it up close to the chest strap sending unit as you would naturally on a run, it simply pops on and gives you your pulse. Not only that, it is so water resistant, you can wear it during a swim workout or a water running session!

The prices have also fallen out of the stratosphere so that just about anyone can afford to get into the same high-tech training concept now in use by many of the top endurance athletes in the world. The list price is $119, but we are offering it for $99.

The other model we carry is also simple, but The Edge allows you to set a "zone," and then beeps at you when you're above or below it. I have to admit, it's pretty handy to have that reminder when you haven't been training a lot, and you're not yet able to gauge effort very accurately. It also has a memory playback feature that tells you what percentage of your workout was spent in the set zone. The Edge normally sells for $189, but we offer it for $159.

Free How-To Booklet

Buy any Polar heart monitor (we carry all models–just call) at our reduced prices, and we'll throw in a copy this this book, *Heart Monitor Training for the Compleat Idiot*, a $4.95 value.

No matter which monitor you use with our easy-to-understand program, you'll be doing cutting edge training in a matter of minutes!

---

*Polar Favor Heart Monitor &
Book*
$99 + $4 shipping and handling
Code: POL

---

*Polar Edge Heart Monitor &
Book*
$159 + $4 shipping and handling
Code: PO2

---

*Heart Monitor Training
for the Compleat Idiot* (book only)
by John L. Parker
paper, ©1993, 64 pgs. **$4.95**
Code: HMT

The Polar Edge   The Polar Favor

Once A Runner
A NOVEL
by John L. Parker, Jr.

How often do you hear about someone borrowing a friend's book, then later buying his own copy because he liked it so much? Or a book so treasured that it gets passed from friend to friend until it simply falls apart from so many readings? *Once a Runner* is such a book.

It has become a cult classic and remains our all-time best seller. It has been acclaimed over the years by Frank Shorter, Bill Rodgers, Alberto Salazar and many other top runners as the best running novel ever. The story of college runner Quenton Cassidy's battle to the top is widely regarded as the most accurate portrayal yet written of the little known world of world class runners.

Many readers say they learned more about running from this novel than from all the training books they have read.

It won *Running* magazine's award as the best book of the year, and has been highly acclaimed by *Running Times, Racing South, and Track & Field News,* as well as by writers like Joe Henderson, Don Kardong and Kenny Moore.

"I've read *Once a Runner* six times and still enjoy it immensely. It continues to renew my heart to 'go after the fire, not the smoke.'"

——**J.A. Sandoz,** Olympia, WA

"Please send me two more copies of *Once a Runner*. It makes an excellent gift to my running friends. It might interest Mr. Parker to know that one [copy] is presently circulating among the members of the München Ost (East Munich) Track Club in West Germany. I had two of their members stay with me as exchange students last year and gave them a copy upon departure. One of them, a 1500-meter man and miler, wrote that his pulse went to 130 during the description of the last race. 'That's *exactly* how it is,' he said. In return

I received a t-shirt from the Greek marathon from Marathon to Athens——an equitable trade. My thanks to Mr. Parker for a great book."

——**Dave Slaughter,** Florence, KY

"I have just finished reading *Once a Runner* and would like to tell you how much I enjoyed it. I am an assistant cross country coach in Jacksonville at Bishop Kenny High School. Our runners are preparing for the state cross country meet in two weeks. As part of this preparation a lot of them are reading *Once a Runner*."

——**James Bryan,** Jacksonville, FL

"Perhaps the best novel ever written about running. There are parts of *Once a Runner* that are pure poetry. I enjoyed it thoroughly and have never read descriptions of what it is to run and race as accurate and compelling as Parker's. . ."

——**Tom Jordan,** *Track & Field News*

"I hate to use a cliche, but I couldn't put it down." ——**Joe Henderson,** *Runner's World*

"I'm jealous. This is very close to the kind of book I've wanted to write for years. . . [Parker] has shown an ability to find that vein that runners have within them, and write about it better than anyone ever has." ——**Don Kardong,** of *Runner's World*

"By far the most accurate fictional portrayal of the world of the serious runner. . . a marvelous description of the way it really is." ——**Kenny Moore,** of *Sports Illustrated*

Once a Runner, the novel
By John L. Parker, Jr.
©1978, paper, 194 pgs. **$9.95**
Code: OAR

RUNNERS
& Other Dreamers

by John L. Parker, Jr.

What really made Jim Ryun tick? Why did Jim Fixx really die? What is the Cinnamon Bun Theory and what does it have to do with Pat Porter, high altitude sickness, and four national cross country championships?

Parker's writing is as powerful as ever and his many readers will find the answers to such questions and a great deal more in his latest work.

This one is destined to become a cult classic like *Once a Runner* and *Runners and Other Ghosts on the Trail*. In fact, this latest collection of Parker's non-fiction pieces contains everything that originally appeared in *Ghosts on the Trail* (now sold out) plus much, much more. Profiles on Jim Ryun, Pat Porter, Barry Brown, Frank Shorter and others. Incisive essays on Courage, Coming Back, The Aging Athlete, and Missing the Poetry, all from his highly regarded *Ultrasport* columns. Lighter moments like "The Great Dragon Run," "The TeeVee Olympics," "Training in Greece," and "Getting Beat by a Woman."

". . .Parker excites and tantalizes the reader. . . Every runner should read this jewel." ----**Ruben Flores**, *San Antonio Light*

". . .a collection of true stories about runners, for runners, by a runner. John Parker knows running from the inside out and knows how to tell a story." —*California Track and Running News*

An Excerpt

A high desert, like a war, is a very good place to find out some things about yourself that you may not have wanted to know.

How you handle it is your business.

It has always been a favorite of Saints and Madmen and Lost Tribes. A lot of people just leave. The Light gets to them. Or the Space. Or something quite a bit less ethereal, such as the way rattlesnakes like to crawl into your sleeping bag to stay warm. The letters back, though, are always wistful:

. . .I was born and raised in Alamosa. I love every inch of the valley and all the happy memories it holds, and yes, even the sad ones. . .

And:

. . .My grandfather settled in the valley not awfully long after the Indians left! Talk about "soul" ----

Mine lies deep in that river land surrounded by the Rockies. . .

Those from a literary magazine called *Alma*, Spanish for "soul," published out of Alamosa, Colorado, a small town on the floor of the San Luis Valley. "Floor" here is deceptive usage. Alamosa is one and one-half miles above sea level. And anywhere you go from here is up. To live in such a place is to break yourself of your oxygen habit.

And there is something else about the high desert, something you think you already know, but which if you haven't been there you can't really *feel*. It is this: the desert doesn't care what kind of hurry you're in or how fast you're going, it's not going to let you get anywhere. You can sit in your rent-a-car going just under a hundred in a perfectly straight line toward the airport at Denver and after a couple of hours you will still be, relatively speaking, in the same place.

You cannot breathe here and you cannot make any progress against the backdrop. It is the long distance runner's most perfectly articulated nightmare.

Pat Porter, a 26-year-old Olympian, a four-time national cross-country champion, voluntarily lives in Alamosa. He *likes* it. Are you beginning to get the idea?

----**From "Rare Atmosphere, Astringent Light"**

Runners & Other Dreamers
By John L. Parker
©1989, paper, 178 pgs. **$9.95**
Code: RDR

For the others, it may have been a race, but for Brad Townes it was a quest for salvation. He had run all the way from death's door and he had lost everything along the way. In the final mile, he had nothing left to lose except the race. You'll find your heart racing right along with the protagonist in this compelling story, beautifully told by a veteran runner.

The grand daddy of all marathons is the backdrop for this exciting story, with the chapters taking you right through the Great Race itself: Brookline to Hopkinton, Hayden Rowe Street, Hopkinton to Ashland to Framingham, Framingham to Natick, Natick to Wellesley, Wellesley to Newton Falls, The Newton Hills, Brookline, and finally Boston. When you finish, you'll feel as if you'd just run the race alongside Bradley Townes!

Reading this book is a great way to prepare mentally and spritually to run Boston.

"I admit it. I couldn't put the book down. I needed to know----did Bradley Townes win? Did he beat Rodgers and Seko in the premier non-Olympic 26-miler----Boston?. . .Tuckman draws you quickly into the Townes' story and his quest for victory over 26 miles and death."
----**Chuck Morris,** *Maine Running*

". . . enough true details and a fast enough pace to please even an envious writer who looked hard for ways to be critical. I read the book in one sitting, which has only happened two other times in the past ten years. . ."----Joe Henderson, *Running Commentary*

An excerpt

Brad could still make out snatches of the radio coverage over the crowd noise. So they still don't know who I am, he thought. They can just call me Mighty Joe from Hannibal, Mo, he chuckled to himself, despite the fire now spreading through his lungs and back muscles.

Twenty yard ahead he could see Seko and beyond him in the distance, Rodgers. In front of Rodgers was only the motorcycle policeman. Now if I can just tie myself to Seko with an invisible cord, and slowly start to pull the son of a bitch in, he thought, just like Bannister did to Landy. He focused on the rhythmically moving shoulders of the Japanese champion, established contact in his mind, and then grimly set about his task.

Rodgers has just passed the 23 mile point, folks, and still looks as loose and easy as he did when he took the lead back on the hills. Seko is behind him but looks tired. And then there's that mystery man. We still don't have. . . . Oh, excuse me. . . . They're trying. . . . Uh, here it is, I have it. I now have the information! Number 2022 is. . . Bradley Townes. . . whose name is not familiar to me. Nor. . . I'm just checking now. . .No? Nor to anyone else on the press truck.

Repeating: Bradley Townes is in third place. He is from Boston. He is 28 years old, and his best previous time is 2:22:35. He is not affiliated with any club and he lists no sponsoring company or product. I hardly need emphasize that he was not included in any of the pre-race publicity information handed out by the Boston Athletic Association. Again, I apologize, but that is all the information that has been released. We are trying to find out more and we'll let you know as soon as we do.

Brad reached the bottom of the hill and now was just three miles out. Twenty-three down and three to go, he thought. Good God! Just give me the strength. He gave Seko a little tug on the cord. . .

Long Road to Boston
by Bruce W. Tuckman
©1988, paper, 169 pgs. **$9.95**
Code: LRB

Awonderful novel about a mysterious, reclusive runner haunting London's Hampstead Heath. And would you believe, A long-running hit.

This enchanting novel was written by Boulderite Paul Christman, editor of the *Running Stats* newsletter. This is one of those hard-to-find books that you will treasure for years.

"Anyone who considers himself (or herself) a hopeless running nut is going to get a serious kick out of it."----*Running Times*

"Great fun to read and the climactic conclusion boldly rewrites running history, and predicts the future as well."
----*Women's Sports & Fitness*

"There are parts of the narrative that are so familiar you'll feel as if you've been caught thinking aloud."
----*Rocky Mountain Running News*

"This book is like a good race: it starts out easy, picks up in the middle, and finishes with a dazzling sprint. Runners everywhere will enjoy it."----**Lorraine Moller**, Olympian

"An exciting yarn that holds the reader to the tape. . ."----**Dick Quax**, Olympian

An excerpt

God dammit! she thought to herself as Christa and a pack of men began to ease by her like a formation of drenched egrets. *You're not slipping by that easily!* Solian tried picking up her knees, but her mind was making a promise her legs couldn't keep. Christa and company evenly receded from her grasp.

Oh, no, not you too! Solian mentally lashed herself as Mary struggled by her 90 seconds later. *I'm going to drop out. . .no,*

got to keep going. . .third woman. . . you can still break 2:50. . .

Minutes later she stumbled to a stop at a feed station just beyond the 38-kilometer mark, gulped a cup of water, then grabbed a sponge and squeezed it over her head. Her first few steps made her feel nauseous. She probably needed some salt, but in the last few miles of a marathon replacement drinks upset her stomach worse than water. Solian could feel the water sloshing around in her stomach and she was getting very dizzy. The sun seemed to be penetrating right through her AUCKLAND UNIVERSITY singlet and navy-blue nylon shorts. *Don't do it! Don't!* Her mind and body were engaged in a contest: the former urging her to keep running, the latter telling her to walk. *Just make it to the 39-kilometer mark. . . you might start feeling better. . . .* But 100 meters later she found herself walking. God, she hated those pitying looks from the spectators when she wasn't doing well.

"C'mon, Solian, only three kilometers to go!" a man supporting himself on two metal arm-braced crutches shouted from the side of the road. Solian felt tears well up in her eyes. Here was a man who would give anything to walk properly, and she was walking when she could still be running. *But, there's no disgrace in saving yourself for another day. Why kill yourself? Walk off the course and admit you just didn't have the miles.* But it was no go: she knew she would have to finish; the man on crutches merely a reminder of what a gift it was to be able to use her legs. Painfully she began to run again. . .

The Purple Runner
By Paul Christman
©1983, paper,   229 pgs.   **$9.95**
Code: PRU

The best writers in the sport of running take up a fascinating subject, the last frontier of long-distance events: races longer than a marathon.

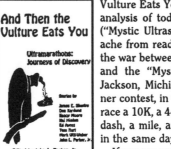

And Then the Vulture Eats You

Ultramarathons: Journeys of Discovery

Stories by
James E. Shapiro
Don Kardong
Kenny Moore
Hal Higdon
Ed Ayres
Tom Hart
Mark Will-Weber
John L. Parker, Jr.

Edited by John L. Parker, Jr.

Who runs these 50-milers, 100-milers, multi-day events, multi-event events? And *why* do they do it? And (okay, admit you're a little curious) what's it like to do one?

James Shapiro, a long time ultra-runner, whose *Meditations from the Breakdown Lane* is a classic piece of running literature, begins by relating with heart-rending detail his experiences in a 6-Day Race in "Swifts on the Wing."

In "To the Limit and Beyond," Kenny Moore takes you through a gut-wrenching experience in his first-person account of the Great Hawaiian Footrace, a horrendous 6-day ordeal that seemingly changes his life.

Don Kardong, one of the wittiest and most personable writers in the sport, in "Le Grizz" goes the 50-mile distance at the infamous race that gives this piece its name. Along the way this former Olympic marathoner, like so many participants in these events, makes startling discoveries about himself.

Ed Ayres, editor of *Running Times*, takes on the Western States 100 in "Wings of Icarus," and the event turns out to be a kind of catharsis in his life.

In "Road Warriors," Hal Higdon's report on his group's informal attempt to run across the state of Indiana is another kind of ultra tale: a light-hearted, self-imposed challenge that turns, like most ultra events, into a revealing spiritual odyssey.

Tom Hart's self-imposed challenge, to run a solo 37-miler on his 37th birthday, is the basis for his ultra story. He finds out, as do the others, that an effort on the magnitude of an ultra is more than a feat of endurance, it is a journey into self.

John Parker ends with "And Then the Vulture Eats You," an uproarious analysis of today's ultra runners ("Mystic Ultras"). Your sides will ache from reading his account of the war between the "Track Men" and the "Mystic Ultras" in the Jackson, Michigan Ultimate Runner contest, in which the entrants race a 10K, a 440, a mile, a 100-yd dash, a mile, and a marathon, all in the same day.

If you are an ultra runner, have ever been even *mildly* curious about such events, or if you are just a lover of great writing, you will greatly enjoy this book.

An Excerpt

From Shapiro's "Swifts on the Wing"
Most of us would be on the track 16 to 18 hours a day. Some would sleep in a trackside tent that swarmed with activity; others like myself would dash off to nearby hotels for a few hours of troubled sleep, tormented by burning feet, sore joints and overtired bodies. Some runners would say much later, when we emerged on the other side of this trial, that they didn't dream about the race while it was actually on but that they did during the first free night.

Certainly there was no way to escape the feverish intoxication of the race. Only once during those six days and nights did the number of competitors sink to just one. At every moment somebody or some bodies moved round the track, ceaselessly at work, so that no matter when you slept, the relentless advance of your competitors seeped through the chill night air, made you awaken with that sobering sense that not another instant could be wasted. It was like war.

And Then the Vulture Eats You
Edited by John L. Parker, Jr.
©1990, paper, 166 pgs. $9.95
Code: VUL

This critically acclaimed novel, first published in 1969, has for years been regarded as one of the true classics not only in the literature of footracing, but in general interest literature as well.

THE OLYMPIAN
By Brian Glanville

Glanville's beautifully portrayed relationship between runner Ike Low and the eccentric and charismatic coach Sam Dee has become a set piece in the tales of athletes: *Rocky, Chariots of Fire,* even *Long Road to Boston* owe a debt to this work.

There are echoes of *Loneliness of the Long Distance Runner* as well. You will be captivated by the story of the working-class stiff, Ike Low, as Sam Dee "discovers" him thrashing through inconsequential races, a mediocre sprinter at a local running club.

"The first time I met him, I thought he was a nut case," said Ike of his coach.

"You are built to run the *mile,*" Dee told him. "You are the perfect combination of ectomorph-mesomorph; long calves, lean, muscular thighs and arms, chest between thirty-seven and thirty-eight, and broad, slim shoulders. A miler is the aristocrat of running. A miler is the nearest to a thoroughbred racehorse that exists on two legs."

And thus begins the relationship that will transform Ike into one of the great distance runners in the world.

"Until *Once A Runner,* this was my favorite running novel." —**Bill Rodgers**

"When I was a miler in college, this book was my *Once a Runner.*" —**John L. Parker**

An Excerpt

This thing, this pain thing, in a way I saw what he meant, but in another way, I didn't understand it. Why run at all if it was going to hurt you? Sport, to me, was something you enjoyed, and if you didn't enjoy it, you packed it in. On the other hand, I could see he was right, that this sort of attitude wasn't going to get you nowhere, not with everybody else so dead serious and more or less dedicating their lives to it. Either you did it properly, or you might as well let it alone.

And mind you, it wasn't like there was no enjoyment in it at all, that it was all slog. The training was hard, of course, and all the things you had to give up, but the races, they could really be great, if things were going well; so exciting that everything else in the world seemed dead; that moment when it was time to go and you felt this power thrumming away in you like a great, big engine and you knew you were going to do it, beat the lot of them. In a way it was better than actually doing it, like a meal or making love to a bird; I mean, it usually looks better beforehand. Though winning was great, too, breaking that old tape, the little, light touch against your chest, and the first feeling you always had, didn't matter how tired you were, was always this flutter in the guts, like to say, I've done it.

The other way I could see Sam was right was obviously if you want something, you ain't going to get it for nothing, not unless you inherit it, and you can't inherit running, and there was a hell of a lot to want in athletics——breaking records, running for Britain, traveling abroad, and maybe one day, please God, an Olympic medal. Because records, they were here today and gone tomorrow, but an Olympic gold medal they could never take away from you.

The Olympian
By Brian Glanville
©1969, paperback, 253 pgs., **$9.95**
Code: **OLY**

This is the wonderful autobiography of Clarence De-Mar, seven-time winner of the Boston Marathon. In an age that had not yet conceived of masters running, his last Boston victory came in 1930 when he was nearly 42!

Marathon

The Clarence DeMar Story

Originally published in 1937, this little gem was nearly forgotten for many years. It was discovered and reprinted in 1981, then forgotten again. Charmingly written in De-Mar's own heartfelt words, it provides a fascinating glimpse into an America of a simpler time.

Perhaps the best-known distance runner of his era, DeMar never profited monetarily from his prowess. He prided himself on his simple New England values: his work as a typesetter, his leadership of a Boy Scout troop, his church work. Much of his training was accomplished during his runs to and from work each day.

He discusses a great many of the unsolicited suggestions about diet, training, and lifestyle he received over the years, a few of which he dutifully tried on himself by way of experimentation. He was a shrewd analyst, open to new ideas, yet with enough skepticism to give weight to his findings. Amazingly enough, *nearly all* the conclusions he reached over 50 years ago about these complex issues have been validated by subsequent research.

In so many ways, DeMar was way ahead of his time. You'll be fascinated by his story.

"Clarence DeMar may have run through----and to the top of----another era, but his story will ring true to all modern marathoners. Today's runners will not only enjoy reading about the way it was; they may even learn a little about the way it should be."

—Amby Burfoot, *Runner's World*

"Long after many of the current running books are forgotten----and deservedly so for some of them----*Marathon* will continue to be in the front of the pack. That's where Clarence DeMar always was himself."

—Colman McCarthy, *Washington Post*

MARATHON by Clarence DeMar
©1937, paper, 156 p. **$9.95**
Code: **CDM**

There has never been another Pre.

Steve Prefontaine, a true American original, captured the imagination of running fans in the 70's like no one before or since. An American record-holder many times over, the charismatic, fearless, outspoken Pre attracted hordes of fans to the University of Oregon's Hayward Field to watch him take on the best in the world. They were called Pre's People. Thousands of others around the world were avid followers of this magnetic personality. They still grieve his tragic death in a 1975 car wreck, just hours after winning his latest 5000-meter race at Hayward.

Jordan covers Pre's meteoric career from his early high school races in Coos Bay, Oregon (where he set a national two-mile record of 8:41.5 in 1969), through his college days racing the likes of Frank Shorter, Kenny Moore, Greg Fredericks, Harold Norpoth, Don Kardong, Lasse Viren, and Rod Dixon. He covers Pre's agonizing fourth in the '72 Olympic final (13:28.3 to Viren's winning 13:26.4), his great '73 and '74 seasons (six American records), and the start of what should have been the greatest racing year of his career.

PRE! by Tom Jordan
©1977, paper, 129 pgs., **$9.95**
Code: **PRE**

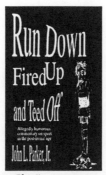

This is Parker's newly revised humor collection, originally published as Aerobic Chic & Other Delusions. This book containns everything in the original, plus eight new hilarious chapters, including "Flo Jo's Folly", "Life Among Skinflints", and classic Parker commentary on runners' gadgets, his trip to Greece, and the sport of cross country.

There is also his classic "Aerobic Chic" quiz the status-seeking runner can take to determine just how "with it" he or she is. (Hint: If you think a Rosa Mota is a new four-cylinder Japanese roadster, you lose 50 points.) Here's a rundown of the other chapters: "Harry Winkler and the Awesome Attack of the Toothless Shark" is about a phony shark attack pulled by some of Parker's skin-diving buddies. "Won't you come home, Irv Taylor?" is the story of an old-timey runner who retires in disgust because of all the newcomers in their

fancy running togs. "Big Stakes at Twin Lakes" is about Parker and a friend running a mile relay against four other guys. "My Latest Marathon" is a survivor's account of his first 26-miler. "Mountain Climbing in Florida" tells of Parker's quest to reach the highest point in his not-so-mountainous home state of Florida. "The Blister Derby" recounts his first and last attempt at race-walking. "Stalking the Wild Pelota" is Parker's side-splitting account of playing Jai Lai for the first and last time.

Needless to say, this is a great gift or back-of-the-john book.

"I laughed till I thought I would have to send out for a truss. . ." —**Ron Wiggins**, *Palm Beach Post*

Run Down Fired Up & Teed Off
By John L. Parker, Jr.
©1993, paper, 80 pgs. **$6.95**
Code: RDF

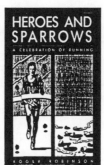

Heroes & Sparrows is a cornucopia of great writing by New Zealander Roger Robinson. Pieces on Joan Benoit, Peter Snell, Dave Bedford, George Sheehan, Carlos Lopes and much much more.

Robinson, a professor of English in New Zealand is a truly fine writer on running, as well as a sub-2:20 masters marathoner. He is also seen from time to time as a television commentator on road races. This book, a rare find that makes a much valued gift, is published in New Zealand and imported to the U.S.

"This book is worthy of the scholar's library, as well as the sports follower's bookshelf." ----**Larry Saunders**, *Christchurch Star*

"A Cambridge education, the ability to

run a sub-2:20 marathon after turning forty, a keen perceptive eye for the unusual, and a love of the sport and its stomping grounds, all contribute to Roger Robinson's ability to write."

----**Paul Christman**, *Running Stats*

"[Robinson's] book is the most scholarly collection of stories and essays I've read on running. It's really great."----**Gary Fanelli**

Heroes and Sparrows
By Roger Robinson
paper, 183 pgs. ©1986 **$16.95**
Code: HER

This is simply the most comprehensive book on endurance training ever compiled. Somewhere in its 832 pages is a discussion of nearly every conceivable topic of interest to the serious athlete. Noakes is a medical doctor and exercise physiologist as well as a long-time runner, with more than 70 marathon and ultramarathon events in his log.

He explores the physiology of running with entire chapters on muscle structure and function, oxygen transport, energy metabolism, and control of body temperature.

You'll discover important new ideas in research, such as recent doubt about the VO2 max concept and its implications for predicting running performance, and the newly realized importance of drinking patterns during exercise in determining fluid and energy replacement.

Noakes considers all aspects of training, offering practical guidelines on shoes and apparel, tips for beginners, and advice on finding the right races for your skill level. He includes fascinating insights from pioneer training theorist Arthur Newton, chapters on training the mind, the problems of overtraining, and the approaches taken by 34 of the world's greatest runners.

Noakes also deals with the down side: injuries and other health considerations. He demonstrates convincingly that injuries don't "just happen," and tells you how to recognize, diagnose, avoid, and treat them. He includes chapters on nutrition and weight control, as well separate chapters dealing with issues relating to both women and children.

Finally, he examines both the benefits and hazards of endurance training as it relates to the body's major systems, including the respiratory, gastrointestinal, genitourinary, endocrine, immune, and central nervous system. He devotes considerable space to environmental hazards, coronary heart disease, longevity issues, and instances of sudden death in athletes.

Dr. Noakes is the Liberty Life Professor of Exercise and Sports Science, and director of the Bioenergetics of Exercise Research Unit of the Medical Research Council of the University of Cape Town. He is an editorial board member for many international sport science journals and the 1991 president of the South African Sports Medicine Association as well as a Fellow of the American College of Sports Medicine.

"Noakes has a training, an intelligence, a sensitivity, and experience that few writers on the athletic life can equal. On every page we see the work of the scientist. . . "
---George Sheehan, MD

Long-time *Runner's World* editor and one of the true veteran commentators of our sport, Joe Henderson, reminisces about how the running boom all came about. This book was unavailable for years and has now been brought back by Cedarwinds. Many insights and helpful suggestions about training, racing, and living the life of a runner.

An excerpt:

I got lucky. First, I was lucky to find running. We were suited for each other, and I have no doubt that it has made me a better person. I don't mean better than anyone else. I don't make those kind of comparisons. I mean better by far than I would have been if I never had started again after dropping out of my first race in April 1958.

Next, I got lucky when I started to write. I learned the craft without really trying. It grew out of record-keeping for running. I learned to write the way I learned to run----by doing it, by building from each day's little defeats and victories until I had a foundation much bigger and stronger than I ever tried or expected to make.

I won state championships in high school, ran miles in the 4-teens, went to college free, traveled the country for races. I wrote for newspapers, magazines, booklets and books. I edited the most important journal in running publishing history. But all the while I knew: It was luck and then persistence that took me there, not talent.

I don't say any of these things to demean myself. I like myself and I'm proud of nearly everything I've done. I'd be a fool to say I didn't enjoy winning seven state high school championships, running four sub-4:20 miles, running in two national cross country meets and competing in almost half the states when I still took racing seriously.

I'd be denying what I am if I said my ego didn't like seeing my byline on top of articles, my name on the front of books, myself being applauded as I stood up to speak, or being asked my advice and opinions---first by letter and phone, and later on radio and TV.

But when I review the things that have given and continue to give me real pleasure, the few big moments aren't anywhere near the top of the list. When I think back on the best day of my running life----May 20, 1961, when I won the Iowa mile and half-mile in record times----it seems it happened to someone else. When I see one of my books on a store shelf, I feel little parental attachment to it. The book was mine only as I wrote it, then I gave it up for adoption.

I get my real pleasure from the words flowing from pen to paper in just the right sequence. I get it from the flow of steps down from my head, through my guts and legs, out through my feet to the good earth.

A no-nonsense approach to the basics of racing on the road, including training. A good first reference work for soeone thinking about racing or inthe early stages of competition. Contains photos and an appendix with pacing charts and metric to yard conversons. Chapters include: The History of Road Racing, Selecting Races, Training for Road Races, Racing, Injuries, and Auxiliary Aids for Runners. The

writers are the well-known University of Oregon women's coach and his athlete/journalist wife.

You know you have the will, but do you have the power to make your best time better?

This book shows you hundreds of practical and exciting ways to punch up your performance on the track, in the gym or, for that matter, on the job.

Dave Scott, 6-time winner of the Hawaii Ironman Triathlon calls it "an invaluable addition to my health library." Thousands of Runner's World readers have turned to Applegate's columns for her insights into an area of the sport that top athletes never neglect, their diet.

A lecturer at the University of California, Davis, Dr. Applegate doesn't promote elaborate diet plans or special products,

"AN INVALUABLE ADDITION TO MY HEALTH LIBRARY."
—Dave Scott, 6-time winner, Hawaii Ironman Triathlon

POWER FOODS

High-Performance Nutrition for High-Performance People

- One-Minute Meals for Maximum Energy
- Recovery Eating after Intense Action
- Vitality Vitamins
- Personalized Eating Plans
- Dozens of Diet tips for improving Athletic Performance

by Liz Applegate, Ph.D.
Nutrition Columnist, *Runner's World* Magazine

rather simple changes in eating styles and food selections that help athletes feel more energetic during workouts, bounce back more quickly afterwards, and otherwise conquer daily challenges that otherwise sap performance.

Find out what trouble spots you may have in eating style and food selection, whether you get too few or too many calories, how to lose weight the high-energy way, what to order at restaurants for improved stamina, how to limit fatigue, and how to power shop at grocery stores.

Power Foods by Liz Applegate
©1991, paper, 288 pgs., **$12.95**
Code: POW

Nancy Clark is perhaps the best known sports nutritionist in the country. She has been a dietary consultant to such sports greats as Olympic figure skater Kitty Caruthers, tennis champ Tim Mayotte, and the Boston Celtics basketball team. Her first book, *The Athlete's Kitchen* was highly acclaimed by coaches and athletes.

Her latest book, sub-titled "Eating to Fuel Your Active Lifestyle," contains 103 fast, practical, and nutritious recipes that are ideal for any sports diet. But this is much more than a recipe book. It features up-to-date information on sports nutrition topics, such as carbohydrate loading, fluid replacement, pre-competition meals, protein needs, and weight loss/gain during training.

The book also includes 43 food and nutrition tables to help individuals determine the best food choices to fit their needs. You'll also find nutrition tips for

Nancy Clark's
SPORTS NUTRITION GUIDEBOOK

Eating to Fuel Your Active Lifestyle

NANCY CLARK, MS, RD
AUTHOR OF THE HIGHLY ACCLAIMED
The Athlete's Kitchen

diabetic athletes, traveling, vegetarian diets and vitamin supplements.

"Drawing from her personal experience as the staff nutritionist for Boston's SportsMedicine Brookline, Clark uses frequent 'Real People' examples to illustrate diet disasters and nutrition makeovers with winning results. . . For nutrition novice and master alike." ----Lynn Detrick, *Cooking Light*

"This books is filled with examples of stock-broker marathoners, college student triathletes, body builder and ice skaters whom she has successfully counseled for various food and nutrition problems." ----*Journal of Nutrition Education*

Nancy Clark's Sports Nutrition Guide by Nancy Clark
paper, 323 pgs. ©1990 $14.95
Code: NCS

This is an enthralling true story of the little-known, reclusive tribe in the mountains of Mexico whose members think nothing of running hundreds of miles at a time. One Tarahumara is known to have run nearly 600 miles in five days to deliver a message. One of the tribe's favorite hunting methods is to chase a deer until it simply drops from exhaustion.

Lutz explores the Tarahumara culture in some detail, including the game of *rarajipari*, in which teams compete by kicking a small wooden ball to a distant goal, sometimes several days away.

This very interesting little book is a quick read and contains sections of interest to children. With its beautifully colored cover and color photographs, it would make an ideal and hard-to-find gift for a

running friend. Forward by Joe Henderson.

"Have the Tarahumara received a special dispensation from some of the human limitations known to us? If they have, I suspect it is because these limitations are artificial. They have been based on our imperfect knowledge of what man can and cannot do."
----**Dr. George Sheehan**

"The Tarahumara may be the finest natural distance runners in the world."
—**Michael Jenkinson**

For ultrarunners as well as us mere 10kers and marathon-ers. This is the fascinating, true story of the legendary Ted Corbitt, a pioneer ultra-distance runner of the 1950's. More than a compelling personal story of a black athlete in a little known sport, this book is also filled with Corbitt's hard-earned wisdom from thousands of miles of training and racing in the "pre-boom" days. Corbitt's courage and determination will enthrall and inspire you. This hard-to-find book makes a great gift.

An Excerpt

The gun barked and they were off. They had to circle the track 3 1/2 times before heading out of the stadium and onto the road.

After two laps Ted noticed a familiar figure cruising alongside him.

The famous facial contortions were missing, but his powerful stride was unmistakable. The "Prague Express" [Emil Zatopek] glided by without effort, gradually moving up on the leaders.

At the head of the long procession, England's Jim Peters cut himself loose from the pack with a devastating burst. Ted's dream of glory ended almost before it began. Leaving the stadium at the fastest pace of his life, he felt an agonizing pain in his right side. It was the worst stitch he had ever known.

Maybe it was the exceptional pace or the terrible tension he had suffered all these weeks. Immediately the pain slowed him and he started losing ground. Yet, despite the stitch he remained with men who would eventually finish in the top ten. Then Jones and Dyrgall swept past. Dyrgall called out, "Watch the pace, it's awful fast." At that moment the pain was at its worst, but even when it eased there was a binding sensation which persisted throughout the remaining distance. . .

Most runners are by now aware of the potential benefits of sports massage. But although there have been a number of books on the more superficial "feel good" massage techniques, there has been precious little available on the deep-tissue work that brings about such profound results with athletes.

Finally, there is a massage book oriented towards athletes. The author is the director of the Chicago School of Massage Therapy, himself a former runner, boxer and weightlifter. He has worked on the likes of Joan Benoit-Samuelson, Chuck Norris, and Mikhail Baryshnikov.

The book is well organized and lavishly illustrated with high quality color photographs, explaining in very clear language most of the effective techniques used by sports massage therapists, as well as the physiological and anatomical basis for these techniques. This is a very helpful book that belongs in the libraries of serious athletes.

Performance Masssage
by Robert K. King, CMT
paper, ©1992, 150 pgs., **$14.95**

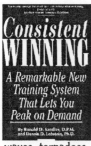

This book describes a peaking system based on the fascinating theory of "Fibonacci numbers," the series of number found in many patterns of nature, such as the nautilus shell, ocean waves, tornadoes, the formations of tree branches, and so on.

The authors contend that human fitness progresses along the same mathematical patterns and demonstrate how to use this concept to accomplish absolute physical peaks when you want to.

"The newest thing I've seen in training in 20 to 25 years." ----**Ray Hosler**, bicycling columnist, *San Francisco Chronicle*

Consistent Winning
by Ronald Sandler & D. Lobstein
paper, ©1992, 122 pgs., **$14.95**
Code: CNS

This is perhaps the most comprehensive book on stretching available today for healthy athletes. This easy-to-follow guide contains illustrated instructions for running as well as 28 other sport-specific stretching routines. Each routine includes 12 best stretches for more than 20 specific sports and recreational activities. Tennis, gymnastics, basketball, the martial arts, swimming, and many other sports are dealt with specifically with regard to proper stretching routines.

You will learn the basic principles, as well as what happens to your bones, joints, tissues, and muscles when you stretch. You'll discover how increased flexibility translates directly into better performance and lessens your chances of injury.

Sport Stretch
by Michael J. Alter
paper, 155 pgs. ©1990 **$15.95**
Code: STR

This book belongs in the library of every serious runner. It is a concise, straightforward guide for the identification and treatment of nearly 100 common sports injuries. Extremely well illustrated with more than 350 drawings and photographs. This is simply the best book on sports injury treatment and prevention we've seen yet. The first time you need quick, practical advice on an injury problem, this book will have paid for itself many times over.

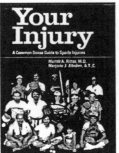

Chapter titles

1. What is an Injury? Sprains, strains, contusions, fractures, etc. ; 2. Proper Immediate First Aid: rest, compression, ice, etc.; 3. Principles of Rehabilitation

4. Environmental Concerns: heat & cold related problems; 5. The Foot: stress and march fracture, heel bruise, bone spurs, etc.; 6. The Ankle: outer ankle sprain, broken ankle, ankle exercises

7. The Lower Leg: shin splints, achilles tendon & soleus-gastrocnemius rupture, etc.; 8. The Knee: inside and outside knee pain, ligament tears, etc.; 9. The Thigh: bruises, contusions, myositis ossificans, etc.

10. The Hip: iliopsoas tendinitis, avulsion fracture, etc.

11. The Abdomen: bruises, strains, stitch, exercises

12. The Thorax: pain in ribs, injury to internal organs

13. The Low Back: disc problems, intervertebral disc syndrome, etc.

14. The Neck: torticollis, wryneck, cervical nerve stretch syndrome, etc.

15. The Shoulder: separation, rotator cuff tear, impingement syndrome

16. The Upper Arm: bruises, strains, tendinitis in upper arm, etc.

17. The Elbow: bicipital tendinitis, hyperextension, lateral epicondylitis

18. The Wrist and Fingers: carpal tunnel syndrome, ulnar tunnel syndrome

> ***Your Injury:***
> by Merrill Ritter, M.D.
> ©1987, spiral, 188 pgs.,**$19.95**
> **Code: YIN**

A truly excellent book on injuries with an emphasis on prevention, cross-training, and the psychological aspects of injuries and their prevention. Written by a whole panel of top trainers, edited by two highly qualified and experienced injury experts. Numerous diagrams and illustrations. Tends to go into more detail than *Your Injury*, particularly with reference to the origins of most injuries, and thus will satisfy the academics among you

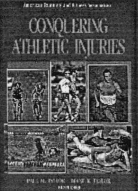

walking wounded. And if it may perhaps tell you a bit more than you wanted to now about a subluxing peroneal tendon, well, maybe having to read about it will remind you not to overdo it the next time.

> ***Conquering Athletic Injuries***
> ed. by Paul Taylor &
> Diane Taylor
> ©1988, paper, 326
> pgs., **$19.95**
> **Code: CON**

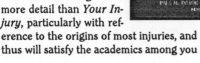

Kenny Moore, aside from being an Olympic marathoner, is perhaps the best crafter of non-fiction prose ever to write on the subject of running.

His book is a continuing source of joy. His style is informative, as befitting a *Sports Illustrated* staffer, yet has the grace of carefully crafted poetry. He zeroes in on such venerable subjects as renowned Oregon coach Bill Bowerman, legendary Aussie record-holder Ron Clarke, first four-minute miler Roger Bannister, and friend and fellow Olympian Frank Shorter.

The classic late 70's mile confrontation between Filbert Bayi and John Walker, multiple gold medalist Lasse Viren, Boston Bill Rodgers, Mary Decker Slaney, Henry Rono, Grete Waitz, Eamonn Coughlan, and Sebastian Coe are all marvelously brought to life by his pen. He writes poignantly of the death of his friend and teammate, Steve Prefontaine in "A Final Drive to the Finish," and recalls the first defini-

tive physiological mass-testing of elite runners (he was one of them) in the early 70's in "Muscle and Blood." There is one piece called "Concentrate on the Chrysanthemums," about one of Shorter's early marathon triumphs, that is worth the price of the whole book.

Moore brilliantly captures some of the most fascinating runners from a particularly interesting era in distance running. This book contains some of the best non-fiction writing ever done on the subject of running.

"This book is delicious. It is ambrosia for the mind."
----**John L. Parker, Jr.**

This is the first book to address in depth the *underpinning* of a successful training regimen. Long-time fitness writer Sleamaker has analyzed the world's best systems of endurance sport training and combined their most effective elements. He deals with principles that apply across all endurance sport boundaries, but also includes sport-specific advice for runners, as well as sections directed at cyclists, swimmers, bi- and triathletes, and others.

"Whether your aspirations are to pursue endurance sports at the local level or to become a world champion, this book is a marvelous resource for analyzing, evaluating, and critiquing your training program."
----**Dave Scott, 6-time Ironman Winner**

FURITURE OR ART?

The "marriage saver" is back!

We were heart-broken, and so were a lot of our customers.

For years, Joan Benoit Samuelson's husband, Scott, has run a company called "Sporting Woods," which made beautiful, artistic furniture pieces for runners.

The lovely, spiraling clothes and shoe stands were the perfect accoutrement for the cluttered runner's apartment or house, and Scott remarked that these products were so effective they reduced a lot of tension in otherwise tempestuous runner relationships.

But suddenly last fall, Sporting Woods announced they would no longer be making the products.

We sulked, we fumed. We would have held our breath and turned blue if it would have done any good.

Then we got the bright idea. We designed our own stand, which we call "The Runner's Rack."

We took the best elements from the low-cost SpiraTree, the all-purpose Sporting Tree, and the sturdy Shoe Stalk, and combined them all into one truly beautiful piece with 14 descending spiral arms for apparel and 8 lower pegs to hold up to 4 pairs of shoes.

Make no mistake; this is a beautifully crafted hardwood furniture item that

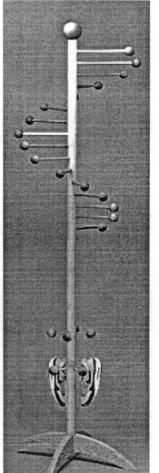

looks more like a work of art. You'll be proud to have it in your home.

Perfect for house or apartment, the Runner's Rack stands over 5 feet tall, is made of 100 per cent solid hardwoods, is naturally stained, and can be assembled permanently with glue, or simply fitted together to allow for later disassembly and packing.

And best of all we kept the price almost as low as the inexpensive SpiraTree. We absolutely guarantee you'll love your Runner's Rack or your money back.

$139 + $6 shipping
Code: RR1

Runners Rack™

Kick Ass Log Software

There are a *lot* of programs out there that will promise to keep track of your training for you. We think *The Athlete's Diary* is the best.

Why? It's easy to use, yet powerful; it does what you want it to, but doesn't overwhelm you with useless bells and whistles. It's smart enough to digest weeks and months of training data and then paint the big picture for you. Plus, it's been around for years, it comes in Mac, DOS, and Windows versions, and it's reasonably priced at $49.95. It's so efficient, you don't even have to have a hard drive. It will run from a floppy. And hey, the manual is written in English!

This program keeps track of times, distances, paces, routes/workout types, and comments. It is also versatile as all get out. You can use it as a straight runner's log, but it'll also handle your occasional cross-training entries. Then when you get injured enough to become a full-time triathlete, you can keep right on using this program–it was actually designed for it. It's billed as "The Computerized Multi-Sport Training Log," and the description fits.

The program allows you to plan your training in advance, print out your workouts, then modify the entries to reflect what actually happened.

Pop-up menus allow you to change your report format from weekly to monthly, from all sports to one sport, and from summary form to graph form. If you really want to *see* how your training has been going, this program will show it to you.

Software designer Steve Jamison is an athlete as well as a computer guy, and his knowledge of training and attention to detail really shows in *The Athlete's Diary*.

Continuing support for the program is provided directly by Stevens Creek Software.

"The Athlete's Diary has provided me with an efficient and user-friendly means of measuring my training progress in order to maximize by athletic potential."

—**Andrew Kelsey,** *Age Group Tri World Champ*

"I would like to say this is one of the most user-friendly programs I have ever used. I am sure there are many more runners that cross-train and are looking for software such as yours. . ."—**Ralph D. Ramos,** *Cincinnati*

". . .works as well with one sport as it does with eight." ——**California Computer News**

". . .does everything but run for you."
——**Running Times**

". . .lots of features, very few weaknesses."
——**Triathlon Today**

The Athlete's Diary
by Stevens Creek Software
©1993, $49.95
Codes: DID (DOS),
DIW (Windows), DIM (Mac)

The Stim-o-Stam Secret

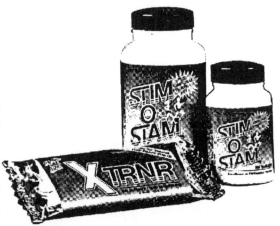

Back in the early days o Track Club in Gainesvi the runners used to notice th what kind of shape you were really hot weather came, you get sore and your training wc suffer. If you were lucky soi might take you aside and let you in on a genuine training secret: Stim-O-Stam. Sounds like some kind of kid's toy or something, but it's really your best defense against hot-weather electrolyte deple-tion and general weariness in all conditions. Marty Liquori and other Gainesville runners have been swearing by it for years. Oh, sure, you could sit around and drink two gallons of Exceed every night, but the truth is that you still prob-ably wouldn't get replenished as well as with Stim-O-Stam. These amazing little tablets are made from a well-guarded for-mula of dibasic and monobasic sodium phosphates, potassium and vitamin C. The company recommends it as a year-around supplement, and says double-blind experiments have shown Stim-O-Stam improves stamina by "main-taining a neutral acid-base balance (pH) in the muscle and blood; making more oxy-gen available; reducing lactic acid build-up, while accelerating ATP production."

The recommended dosage is three tab-lets before, three tablets after workouts, but as many as 12 per day may be taken in extreme heat or workout conditions.

The Xtrnr sports bar is a new product that combines the basic Stim-O-Stam phosphate formula with the fructose, glucose polymers, and branched chain

amino acids needed for no-nonsense ath-letic refueling. Frankly, this honey-nut flavored bar is not as palatable as the PowerBar, its nearest competitor (prob-ably because the phosphate ingredients themselves don't taste all that great), but it offers the same nutritional value of PowerBar with the added electrolyte re-placement benefit of the Stim-O-Stam phosphate formula built in. This is an incredibly powerful product for hard-core performance support and enhancement, not a trendy snack item.

Please specify flavors: Honey Nut, Ba-nana Nut, or Chocolate Toffee.

Stim-O-Stam tablets (500 tab bottle, 4-6 month supply) $27.95 + $4 shipping
Code: ST1

Xtrnr Sports Bar (24-pack) $39.95 + $4.00 shipping
Code: ST2

Still the old champ

The highly compact design made the old *Runner's Log* a favorite since 1981. Now an updated, even more feature-filled version has been released with Bill Rodgers' imprimatur. At 8½ X 5¼, it's almost small enough to slip into a back pocket, yet features nice thick, card-stock type pages. If you're not into verbose entries and are looking for a really efficient design, this log's for you. Features: 1) Undated; 2) One week per page; 3) Daily slots for course, distance, workout type, time, temperature and humidity; 4) weekly slots for total mileage, week's average, cumulative. 5)3 comment lines per day; 2 for week; 6) handy mood symbols, weight section; 6) Short sections on training tips;

7) Yearly records include: races, mileage graph by the week, cumulative mileage graph; 8) pace charts for two miles through marathon

> ### Bill Rodgers' Classic Running Log by Jogalite
> ©1993, spiral paper, 86 pgs. **$9.95**
> Code: LG7

The contender

Sports Log Publishers puts out some of the most popular logs in sports. Their Runlog is compact at 6" X 9", and nicely laid out, with inspiring color and black & white photographs. Features: 1) Undated pages; 2) Two pages per week, total of 56 weeks; 3) Open format with plenty of room for daily notes 4)

Weekly summary section, with body weight, cumulative mileage and weekly mileage; 5) Short sections on stretching, nutrition, training, etc.; 6) Pace charts, Race result summary log, Map to Race Day Worksheet, and Cumulative Mileage Chart.

This is the one for the verbose runner who's tired of writing in the margins of all his/her past logs.

> ### RunLog
> by Tim Houts & John Cronin
> ©1994, spiral paper, 166 pgs. **$9.95**
> Code: LG1

If anyone should know how to approach training as a masters runner, it's Hal Higdon. The author of *On the Run from Dogs and People* (and 23 other books) covers it all, from the question of health dangers to base training, minimizing injuries, masters secrets, motivation, diet, and maintaining your youth. Higdon, a Senior Writer for *Runner's World* and a contributor to many other magazines, is perhaps the first athlete ever to hold national records in the junior, open and the masters divisions. He has participated in six Olympic Trials.

This book has already been widely praised.

Mike Davis of the *Indianapolis News* wrote: ". . .it's tough to read the first chapter and not get an urge to slip on a pair of shoes and go for a run."

Maurice Hobbs of the *Minneapolis Tribune* wrote: "It would have been nice to have had Higdon's newest book 12 years ago when I started running."

Masters Running Guide
by Hal Higdon
©1990, paper, 144 pgs. **$9.95**

Two of the great masters runners of our times (with the help of *Runner's World's* Joe Henderson) have put together a truly comprehensive, informative, and interesting book on after-40 running. They not only tell you some of their personal backgrounds, but also give you some feel for masters running historically. Did you know, for instance, that Clarence DeMar won the 1930 Boston Marathon at age 41 and is still its oldest winner? Or that 47-year-old Finn Vaino Muinonen won a silver in the European Championship Marathon in 1946? Or that Evy Palm of Sweden PR'd with a 2:31:05 at age 47?

John Campbell, Joyce Smith, Jack Foster, and Miki Gorman are all accorded their proper place in the constellation of masters stars.

The book also gets into the nitty-gritty of training for the mature runner: "What the Years Give to Performance, and What They Take Away"; "The New Way to Train without Injury"; "Nutrition Advice to Keep You Running Smoothly"; "Racing: How to Start, How to Finish"; "Breaking Personal Records"; "What it Takes to Make It Through a Marathon"; "Mastering the

Mile"; and "The Joy of Training and Racing Cross Country" are among the many topics covered. The book also provides handy pacing charts, record listings, and training charts.

The authors hardly need introduction. Rodgers is a four-time winner of both the New York and Boston marathons. At 43 he is now one of America's top masters runners. Welch, now 46, began running at age 35. Within four years she made the British Olympic team and in 1987 won the New York City Marathon. Henderson is the author of 13 books on running and fitness and has been running himself for more than 30 years.

Whether you're training for your first 5K, or planning your umpteenth marathon, you'll not only enjoy your first read of this jam-packed book, you'll keep it handy for future reference.

Masters Running and Racing
by Bill Rodgers & Priscilla Welch
hardcover, 192 pgs. ©1991 **$16.95**
Code: MRR

University of California's track and cross-country coach Vern Gambetta lays out personal background, best marks, annual progression, and both competitive and non-competitive season weekly schedules along with a narrative description of each woman's approach to training.

Women included are: Kathy Adams, Tena Anex, Evelyn Ashford, Diane Barrett, Joan Benoit, Karen Bridges, Ruth Caldwell, Fran Castro, Carol Cook, Kris Costello, Doreen Ennis, Eryn Forbes, Linda Goen, Ellison Goodall, Jennie Gorham, Judy Graham, Doris Brown-Heritage, Lynne Hjelte, Tara Hobbs.

Also: Pam Jiles, Maggie

Keyes, Deby LaPlante, Sue Latter, Sandra Levinski, Wendy Koenig-Knudson, Susi Meek, Molly Miller, Deborah Mitchell-Pearson, Molly Morton, Sue North, Jan Oehm, Phyllis Olrich, Debbie Quatier, Cindy Schmandt, Jarvis Scott, Grete Waitz, Leann Warren, Kathy Weston, Cheri Williams.

One of the most experienced and accomplished writers in the sport takes on the subject of getting better results in the shorter races.

Higdon explains: "While numerous books told people how to start jogging and how to finish their first marathon, less attention is paid to running short races faster. Many of the millions of participants in the current fitness boom skipped high school track and cross-country, where they might have learned the necessary skills. They didn't run in college, either. As a result they missed the training you get at that level. They never learned to warm up properly. They don't have a coach. They don't know about interval training, fartlek, and bounding drills."

This book fills that gap, and does it in Higdon's familiar highly readable, highly personal style. This book covers just about

everything the intermediate runner needs to know to start running faster in races shorter than the marathon.

"Vintage Higdon. He brings perspective to his discussion and demonstrates every point with a story from his own experience or that of other runners, coaches and scientists. A wealth of information." —**David L. Costill, PhD**, author of *Inside Running*

Shipping Rates
(please add to your order form)

Type of Service	FIRST BOOK	EACH ADDITIONAL
Standard Book Rate U.S. Mail	$3	$.50
Priority Mail in U.S. (delivery in 3-4 days)	$4	$1
UPS Ground	$4	$.50
UPS 2nd Day	$7	$1
UPS Overnight	$12	$4
Canada & Mexico Surface	$4	$1
Air Mail	$5	$2
Other Western Hemisphere Countries Surface	$4	$2
Air Mail	$6	$3
Europe Surface	$4	$2
Air Mail	$8	$6
Asia, Africa, Pacific Rim, etc. Surface	$4	$2
Air Mail	$10	$8

Cedarwinds Publishing Company
P.O. Box 351, Medway, OH 45341
Credit Card Orders only:
800-548-2388
Hours: 9 am to 6 pm EST
(or use recording after hours)
Information: 513-849-1689
FAX Orders: 513-849-1624
(Prices subject to change without notice.)

Editorial Offices:
Box 13618, Tallahassee, FL 32317
904-224-9261 fax: 904-561-0747

Quantity	Title	Amount

(Note: Shipping is already added in price of non-book products) Sub-total	
Florida and Ohio residents please add 7% sales tax	
Standard Shipping: Add $3 for first book, $.50 for each additional	
Special Shipping, please specify from box at left:	
TOTAL ENCLOSED $	

NAME_____

ADDRESS_____

CITY_____STATE_____ZIP_____

Important: please furnish telephone numbers below in case we need to contact you.

Day phone: _____

❏ Check or money order enclosed (do not send cash)
❏ Visa/MC

Card No._____

Expiration _____
Signature _____

To order by mail, send check, money order, or
credit card authorization above----payable in U.S.
funds----to:
Cedarwinds Publishing Company
P.O. Box 351— 1305 Park Dr.
Medway, OH 45341

FAX: 513-849-1624
Phone Orders: 800-548-2388

Quantity	Title	Amount

	Sub-total	
(Note: Shipping is already added in price of non-book products)		
Florida and Ohio residents please add 7% sales tax		
Standard Shipping: Add $3 for first book, $.50 for each additional		
Special Shipping, please specify from box at left:		
TOTAL ENCLOSED $		

NAME_____

ADDRESS_____

CITY_____STATE_____ZIP_____

Important: please furnish telephone numbers below in case we need to contact you.

Day phone: _____

❑ Check or money order enclosed (do not send cash)
❑ Visa/MC

Card No._____

Expiration _____
Signature _____

To order by mail, send check, money order, or
credit card authorization above----payable in U.S.
funds----to:
Cedarwinds Publishing Company
P.O. Box 351— 1305 Park Dr.
Medway, OH 45341

FAX: 513-849-1624
Phone Orders: 800-548-2388